1

4

TREASURES FROM HEAVEN

PROPHECIES OF
CHRISTOPHER WICKLAND
VOLUME 1

6

Special thanks

I would like to say a big thank you to my wife for painstakingly putting commas in the correct places on this manuscript.

A big thank you to Yvonne Coombs for allowing me permission to use one of her beautiful prophetic paintings for the cover of this book.

I would also like to say thank you to Geoffrey Pick from the Prophetic Releasers group on Facebook, for all the years of encouragement you have given me with the prophetic.

A big thank you to all those who have helped and supported me over the years…you know who you are.

Finally thank you Jesus, for taking me on this wonderful and exciting journey into the unknown. Everyday is a life of new wonders with you

8

Treasures from heaven

Copyright 2023 by Christopher Wickland

Published by Amazon

All Rights reserved. No part of this publication may be reproduced, stored in a retrieval system, or transmitted in any form by any means, electronic, mechanical, photocopy, recording, or otherwise, without the prior permission of the author.

Cover artwork Yvonne Coombs. With permission. 2023

First printing 2023

Scripture references marked NASB taken from the NEW AMERICAN STANDARD BIBLE, Copyright 1960, 1962, 1968, 1971, 1972, 1973, 1975, 1977, 1995 by the Lockman Foundation. Used by Permission. All rights reserved.

Scripture references marked ONMB taken from The One New Man Bible, copyright 2011 William J Morford. Used by permission of True Potential Publishing, inc.

Other scriptures taken from the Christian Community Bible. 66th Edition, Revised 2013. Used by Permission. All rights reserved.

11

Endorsements

"Amongst prophetic voices, Chris Wickland stands tall in his boldness and accuracy in revealing future events ahead of time. Chris brings clear prophetic calls, preparing us spiritually and practically. The prophetic words make engaging reading, and are an essential guide for Christians facing challenging times ahead with looming war and famine already unfolding. Yet out of the chaos, a spiritual transformation is coming, sparking revival on a scale never before seen."

Geoffrey Pick of Prophetic Releasers UK.

"Although I live in Australia, I have a burning passion from the Lord for the Uk. On our recent ministry trip to England, my husband and I had a divine set up with Chris Wickland one summer afternoon in South Hampton. Several hours passed effortlessly as we shared our prophetic sensing for the nations and for the UK. What strikes me the most about Chris is that he is not afraid to speak truth and release the deep groanings of the spirit. Some prophets would shy away from this in preference for "candy cane" words and empty encouragements that are not grounded in truth- but not Chris! His words over years have proven accurate and I believe this book is an important resource that can be used to process what God is saying to His people. Take it and open your bible and journal, and ask Him what your part is to play in seeing His kingdom come to the Uk! Thank you Chris for providing this resource with unashamed boldness that reveals the tender heart of our lion, Jesus!"

Roma Waterman
Founder, HeartSong Prophetic Alliance
Award winning songwriter, author

"Chris is a respected Christian leader and someone who has clearly cultivated an intimate walk with the Lord through daily rhythms of prayer. Consequently the prophetic words that he receives are worthy of careful and prayerful attention as we see the culmination of this age. I also believe Chris is one of the humble fore-runners who the Lord has raised up in the UK at this key juncture in human history, so I encourage readers to give careful and prayerful consideration to the prophetic words contained within this book and seek the Lord's guidance and wisdom for the application.

These are the most exciting days to be following Jesus as we see the culmination of this age unfold before our eyes. The Lord is using Chris quite powerfully to prepare us for the glorious re-union"

Rev. Matt Timms –
Wave House Church Lead

Contents

13. Introduction.
15. Rushi Sunak and the Titanic.
17. The Rise of the prophets.
19. The Jenga block.
23. Lament for Oceangate.
25. Awake, awake O Zion.
27. The end but not the end of the established churches.
31. War is coming!
35. I AM your song.
37. The days which are coming.
39. Adonai is mustering an army for war.
41. A taunt song to Stonewall.
43. Jerusalem O Jerusalem.
45. Get ready to enter the promised land.
47. The rending of the cloth.
49. The stained glass window.
51. The changing of the guard.
53. Oh My Church of England.
55. The tide and waves of My Spirit.
57. The knights of the round table.
61. My remnant.
63. My prodigals shall return.
65. My people are asleep.
69. Dream of the shakings to come.
73. The enemies plans will backfire.
77. The three blessings and the three woes.
83. The English oak.
85. The seasons are shifting.
99. Signs in the sun.
103. Visions pertaining to the end of days.
113. Brexit and warnings and blessings for Great Britain.
127. God will restore the broken and lame.
129. God is calling us to the wilderness.
131. I also have sheep that are not of this sheepfold.
135. The marrying of the two great houses.
137. The cutting down of the Sycamore Gap Tree.

Introduction

Dear reader, what you have in your hands is a small selection of prophetic words and sermons that I believe God has given me from over the last five years.

For over twenty years I have received various dreams, words and visions of future events some of which have now already come to pass. Yet, so many others are still pointing to the times in which we live now. I believe we are at a momentous point in history for the nation of the United Kingdom. I believe that God will chastise this nation for the grievous sins she has committed, yet in that chastisement we will see His tender grace and compassion. I believe that in this nation's darkest hour, we will see God move in wonderful ways and I believe He will re-establish His remnant church. Once again we will see Christendom flourish throughout this nation.

Most of the prophetic words and visions in this book are from the last five years and are relevant for the season which lies ahead for the land of Great Britain. I have taken the time to compile these words, some are transcripts of sermons, others are prayerfully considered impressions and words which I believe the Lord laid on my heart.

The prophetic words come in varying types from the comforting and pastoral through to the predictive and serious. My hope is that this small book will give you hope and some clarity for the future of this nation. My prayer is that this little book will cause the church to once again become a praying church and seek God's hand and His revival for our fallen nation for the dark days which lie ahead.

Christopher Wickland 29th of September 2023

Rushi Sunak and the Titanic

RISHI SUNAK you are likened to Captain Edward John Smith the captain of the Titanic. A British made ship that was declared unsinkable. Indeed he was rumoured to have said "Even God himself couldn't sink this ship."

Rishi Sunak you are such a man as this. You think because of your great career and understanding of economics that you are a man worthy to sail Great Britannia through the difficult seas ahead. But you are a man that is the last of your party to lead this country at this time. I am calling time on Britannia's economy, politics and state religion. You have all been deemed wanting and severely lacking.

You have mocked my ways and trampled in the dirt that which was given to this nation and the favour she once carried. Oh HMS Britannia your days are numbered now. Your politics will become a shock and laughing stock to the world, the collapse of your economy will be brutal and the fall of your state religion will make many nations gasp in surprise and shock. The pride of Britannia will be brought low. She will lose so much of her favour which she once enjoyed.

Yet, I will stay my hand as the church rises up to pray for this nation and then I will turn from my anger and be tender to this nation again. I will raise her up to be a sheep nation to be a blessing to others.

Britain will be for a short period of time a safe haven from the Great War that is coming. During this time of favour the church will blossom and grow strong over this nation.

I will restore a better government that is humble before me, I will give Britain back a working economy but it will be weaker than today. I will also raise up the state church from its demise.

Yet this will all be for a season before the last of days comes to play. You have a generation left. Use this time wisely church. Get ready to intercede for this nation. Get ready for a massive crop to be gathered into the barns. Time is running out fast. You are so close to the end of days you all need to wake up. And yes even those who claim to be awake are asleep at the helm. Wake up, O sleeper, wake up my sleeping beauty.

Chris Wickland 17th of June 2023

The Rise of the Prophets

Exodus 16:15b '... *"it is the bread which Yahovah has given you to eat."*

I have given bread for my church to eat. I have given her manna from heaven on high. I have supplied her with heavenly food and sustained her through the wilderness of the last 40 years. The wilderness has been costly and difficult for my church. Yet great struggles still await ahead. But this time the struggle will not be to survive in the wilderness and barren lands. No, this time I want my people to be established again and to settle into a promised land. The promised land of revival, renewal and reformation.

Yet this revival will not be like previous moves of my sacred, set apart and Holy Spirit. No, this revival will be as a woman in labour. Great travail is coming for this nation of Great Britain, great shakings are coming to this land of Nod. (As Israel was in Egypt and in Babylon, so they became a great and respected people, for my signs and wonders was with them, for I was with them.) So I too will be with my church with great signs and wonders in the days ahead.

During these days, you will see Josephs, Daniels, and Esthers arise within the church and within the secular world. These are my chosen vessels to be a blessing to my church and to be a mercy to those who do not yet know my Name.

Deuteronomy 8:3b '...man shall not live by bread alone, but man lives by every word that proceeds from the mouth of Yahovah.'

The voice of the prophets will be necessary in those days to navigate the tempestuous waters ahead. Old church models that are blind prophetically will struggle and fail. This will be grievous to me. Man will need to listen to my 'Now!' Word to understand the signs of the times. The church will need to become an Issachar generation, a people of the time who understand the times in which they live.

However, in the days ahead I will be raising up prophetic voices the likes similar to Samuel. Their words I will not allow to fall to the ground. They will be accurate, sharp and on point. I will raise up great spiritual giants in this land of the UK to be a strong prophetic voice to help my church, my beloved people through what's coming. These will be voices that you will learn and grow to trust and accept and love. These prophetic giants will be few but there will be men and women prophets, some old and seasoned, some young and fiery.

My church cannot simply live by bread alone in the days ahead, but she must live by the spoken word of God. Often My people perish for lack of knowledge. In the days ahead you will need clarity in ways you have not needed before. This is why the office of prophet will be elevated and established in the days ahead.

Get ready my church for the greatest seismic shift ever experienced in modern times, and be watching and praying and listening for those voices who are soon going to be raised to great prominence. These are voices I will raise up, these are not voices men will choose to raise.

Chris Wickland 19th of June 2023

The Jenga Block

Hosea 4:6 *'My people perish for lack of knowledge…'*

Oh my church how I love you my people. How I long to cover you with the pinions of my wings and overshadow you with my love and tenderness.

I need you to understand my church that I first of all love you with such a tender love, such a passionate love, such a jealous and consuming love. You are the apple of my eye and I am devoted to you My church.

I bring you this message my love as a warning for you to be ready, to beware and be forearmed for what is coming. My people have grown dull to my words in these days. I have sent warnings and signs and they have been missed by my own people as nothing but mere coincidence. My people I love you, but you have become hard of hearing and dull of heart. So that, in seeing, you no longer see. In hearing, you do not always hear and in perceiving, your heart has become dull. I am left with little choice but to spell this out to you my people in a way that you can see, hear and perceive.

You live in the land of the United Kingdom, a land that is now under the shadow of my chastisement. All that can be shaken will be shaken, but you my love, my church, are of a kingdom that cannot be shaken. I do not want my people to be swept away by what is coming. NO! I want her to stand strong in the days ahead and be a lighthouse to the nations, to the Gentiles. A lighthouse to your communities and your neighbours.

My lovely people, my church, my bride to be, hear me. I am about to pull the 'Jenga Block,' on your economy that will bring it all crashing down. Your nation has become rebellious, fat, proud and has turned her back on me. She has passed Ordinances, Statutes and Decrees that are in violation to my own. I have given this land time to repent but she has not done so, rather she has hardened her heart toward me even more.

Therefore, my people I give you a stark warning. You have the remainder of this year and the next to get ready and prepared for what is about to come. When my prophet Agabus gave a prophecy (Acts 11:27-30), my church in that day heeded his warning.

I give another such warning. There is coming a financial famine the likes never seen in modern history. It is a famine that will bring down the lies, filth and degradation of this nation. However, if you my lovely people are not ready then you may be swept away in fear and surprise by what is coming. If you do not prepare now, then you will not be able to prepare at all.

Joseph was raised in his day to protect my people from famine. Whilst I gave years of plenty there was time to store and fill the barns with grain. Sadly your years of plenty are over and the famine is now beginning to take the land slowly but surely.

You have one and a half years left to make preparations for what is coming ahead. You need to pray about this and test this and discern what you need to do as a community. For once the allotted time is up, it will then be too late to do any meaningful preparation.

The Jenga Block will be a keystone in your current fragile economy. I will pull the block from under the housing market and with that will come the toppling of great institutions that will usher in a great famine over this land.

Many will read this word, some will be perplexed, some worried, others will laugh and scoff whilst others will seriously pray, weigh and test. I will permit the word to go far and wide and be a wonder to many.

Sadly there are many who will only heed this message when they finally see with their eyes what is written in this word, but sadly it will be too late to do anything of meaningful value.

I bring this message to you to console you my church, to adjure you, and give you hope. If you can stand in the time of famine, then you will stand strong and my Spirit and miracles shall surely be with you.

Be like Samson, do all you can with all your might and I will do the rest. In those days I will perform great miracles of provision also. So do the best you can and I will compensate for what is lacking. Remember the name Joseph means, 'I will add to that which is lacking.'

Be encouraged my people; during this famine will come a great spiritual harvest. So be ready and prepared. Be ready in the natural and ready in the spiritual.
I love you my people, I love you and want you to stand strong.

Chris Wickland 21st of June 2023

Lament for Oceangate

This was given while searching for the Titan mini sub that went missing near the Titanic

How lonely sits the Oceangate in the depths of the earth.
How you went to the deep like my servant Jonah
Like a poor widow, many grieve your passing.
Many lament for you, poor Oceangate.

As the world looks on and grieves for you,
I have set you as a sign, a wonder and a riddle,
Like the great Titan, I have brought the pride of nations low.
Down deep into the depths,
at the feet of those who have gone before.

Oceangate, Oceangate, how people morn your passing.
You will not be forgotten, forever a word of warning
You now dwell among the others of the deep.
Among the dead you shall sleep.

Wealth, prestige and honour are no match for my ocean.
In the vastness of my sea, man learns his place
Oceangate, how you have been brought low.
Oceangate how you have fallen.

Lament her passing, lament the loss
Lament her well, oh nations above.
Learn from this my people
Learn from this tragic loss.

Look and ponder, o world above
For Oceangate is a sign and wonder.
Secrets of the depths she saw
And now she rests on ocean's floor.

Chris Wickland. 21st of June 2023

Awake, Awake O Zion

Isaiah 52:1. *'Awake, awake, put on your strength, O Zion; put on your beautiful garments, O Jerusalem, the holy city.'*

Awake, awake my beautiful one, my beautiful one. Time to arise from your slumber, sloth and rest. Arise and shine for your light has come my people, it is time to stand up as the Lord your God has stood up.

Can you not hear the sound in the camp? Can you not see the commotion? The Ark of the Covenant is on the move and it's starting to be carried aloft. Therefore arise my people, rise, for my Presence is returning to you, my power and strength is returning to you.

Put on your priestly garments my people, put on your beautiful priestly robes. It's time to minister to the Lord your God, it's time for you to now consider this. Put on those ministering robes and do homage before me.

Put down the things you have been doing and pay attention, for the Ark of the Covenant is on the move. Don't let it pass you by unnoticed. Put down what you are doing and do homage before Me. For my passing is coming and I am in the camp of my people.

My Church, My Church, your garments are in tatters. You are wearing clothes that have long worn out. Your garments of old need to be thrown away. The Ark of my Presence will soon be passing by and you need to be ready, for the passing of your Great and Mighty King is coming.

Sound the shofar, sound it loud for the Ark is being taken out into the people of God. Listen to the voice of my shofars, the prophets, they are heralding my moving. Hear the sound of the shofars and perceive and understand. Is it a call for war? Is it a call for the camp to move? You will only know if you listen to the sound of my shofars.

Commotion is in the camp, excitement is coming to the camp, for the Lord your God is on the move. Wake up, change your soiled garments, put on your priestly vestments. Bathe yourselves and make yourselves clean before Me. Heed the sound of the shofars, understand what is required for the camp and get ready to move. The camp is about to move. I am about to move and lead my people out.

Get ready my people, your time in the wilderness is at an end. Do not gird for war in the armour of Saul in these days. No, put on your ephod and priestly garments for this is your garments of war. Awake My people, arise. For the Ark of the Covenant is on the move.

Chris Wickland 22nd of June 2023

The end, but not the end of the established churches

Amos 8:2b-3. "'The end has come for my people; I will never again overlook their offences. When the time comes, the songs in the temple will be wailings," says Adonai ELOHIM. "There will be many dead bodies; everywhere silence will reign."

Oh apostate church, you who have left the anchor of My truth. You who are cowardly at heart and weak-kneed. You who spin and capitulate to the dance of the world.

Oh apostate church, some of you used to be mine, whilst others never loved Me. Why did you turn from Me? Was I not good enough for you and to you? Yet I hear you say, "How Lord have we turned from you? We still honour you, we still call ourselves by your Name."

Oh apostate church, you honour me with your lips, but your heart is far from Me. You pay lip service to me, but deep inside your heart is rotten to the core. You break my heart with your ways, the ways of a harlot. You look to the world for your so called just causes. You seek them out and flirt with them like a harlot seeking a lover.

Do you think I delight to speak like this? Do you think I want to talk to you like this? You trample on my Word as though it were trash. You twist it, break it and render it null and void with your hypocrisy and so called wisdom.

I have given you time to repent of your deeds. I have allowed you much grace and many days for you to change. My heart is that you would change and turn from your wicked ways and come back to me. Although you are apostate, I still yearn that you would turn back to Me and follow My truth.

The time for your sins is almost up, the bowls filling up are almost complete. Yet I am calling time on you now. I will not allow your ways to further influence and infect my weak ones in the faith. You will no longer be permitted to gain more converts to your cause. You profane my sabbaths, you profane my word, you profane the buildings which are devoted to me with your harlotries and adulteries.

Therefore I will make a sign of you to the nations. Many will shake their heads with shock and disbelief. You will be a proverb and a byword of warning to those around. I will not tolerate the sins of Jezebel in my church any more. Therefore I call time now on all Jezebel churches that claim to be of Me but are not.

It breaks my heart that I now have to call time on the established institutions that claim to be of Me in this land of Britain. I will chastise you and great will be your pain. I will do to you what you least expect, I will pull your strength and your power away from you. You who have the ear of power will be rendered mute. If you can no longer speak for Me and My truth, then you will not be permitted to speak at all.

I see those within you who are mine, I have marked them and I see them. One day, some of those marked ones within whom you have marginalised and silenced, will come back and be the ones I use to raise your institutions back from the grave.

As for you apostates who lead My people into error. Your time has been called. I know very well what you are up to. I see your heart even though you think I do not. You will all fall, and none shall remember you. Your names will not be great as some of you have hoped. No, I will make you forgotten, like smoke in the wind.

I speak now to those whose hearts have been rent and broken over my apostate ones. I have seen your tears and heard your many prayers. I have seen how you stood up for Me even when it cost you so much. I want to comfort you my people with these words. Firstly, you are remembered and your names are written in heaven for being those who stood up for Me and My word. Secondly, I will bring back that which you love so much. Yes, there will be a season of chastisement and I will rid the institutions of those wicked men and women. But night will pass and dawn will rise and healing will be in my wings and I will heal and resurrect that which I put down. I will bring back that which you so love and so cherish.

I love you My people, I love you with an everlasting love. Stay true to Me, keep your ways straight. I will never fail or forsake you. Just remain true to Me, for I am a jealous God and I will have no others before me.   For those who have ears to hear, let them hear what is being said to the churches.

Chris Wickland 26th of June 2023

War is coming!

1 Samuel 14:6. *Johnathan said to his armour bearer, "Come on, let's go across to the garrison of these uncircumcised people. Maybe ADONAI will do something for us, since ADONAI can rescue with a few people as easily as with many.'*

The days of Saul have been numbered. The season of Saul always starts well but sometimes goes astray. To be a man or woman who loves me is not enough to be one who leads my people. Many Pastors in this day have been Sauls. Men and women who love me, yet lean on their own understanding. Saul is great at strategy and war craft, but his emphasis is always on his own strength and his own abilities, he doesn't think to look to Me for wisdom, counsel and might. Such things would be considered foolish to Saul. Saul is one who fears man and his opinions. He capitulates to the pressures of man instead of following in my ways.

1 Samuel 13:8-9. *'Saul waited seven days, as Samuel had instructed; but Samuel didn't come to Gilgal; so the army began to drift away from him. Saul said, "bring me the burnt offering and the peace offerings," and he offered the burnt offering.'*

When the pressure is on, Saul will justify his ends, even when it violates my word, written or prophetic.

1 Samuel 13:13-14. *'"You did a foolish thing. You didn't observe the commandment of ADONAI, which He gave you. If you had, ADONAI would have set up your kingship over Israel forever. But as it is, your kingship will not be established. ADONAI has sought for Himself a man after His own heart, and ADONAI has appointed him to be prince over His people, because you did not observe what ADONAI ordered you to do.'*

I am taking away the kingdom from My Sauls and giving it to My Jonathans and the Davids. I have seen how over the last thirty years many Sauls have hounded and tried to put down the Jonathans and the Davids. You have sought them out and oppressed and suppressed them. Because like Saul, you saw something in them which you knew you lacked. You considered them to be dangerous for you.

Yes some of them were young, immature and underdeveloped in maturity. Yes many of them were rough around the edges. But Saul, you were to bless them, and train them up. You were supposed to teach them your strengths and abilities that it may help them overcome their shortcomings. In Fairness some Sauls have done the right thing and trained and equipped my Davids.

A war is coming, the likes never seen before in modern days. The enemy will be considered a giant to many, too strong and too powerful to topple. The might of Saul will simply not prevail in these days. Only those with the spirit of Caleb, Joshua, Jonathan, David, Esther and Deborah will prevail in the days ahead.

For it is not by might, nor by power but by My Spirit. (Zechariah 4:6). In the days ahead I will pour out My Spirit for My people to do exploits. Some shall run through a troop, leap over a wall or slay the Goliaths of the day. But the ways of Saul will simply not work or suffice in those days.

I need My people to be daring, to be bold, to expect me to move as they run and charge the enemy as David did to Goliath. (1 Samuel 17:48)

These are the days of Elijah. These are the days of mighty prophets and great leaders to arise. My church needs shepherds and my church requires mighty men and women who are valiant in the realms of faith and prayer to lead my people to battle.

It is time to take the promised land. It is time to take the land for me and reinstate my statutes and ways over this nation again as it once was. This battle will be long and it will be arduous, it will take a generation to reinstate that which was lost.

This nation needs to be ready and come back to how she once was if she is to be ready for the last days and face off the rise of the antichrist and his beastly worker of miracles. The sands of time are slipping away, but as the top of the hour glass runs out, the bottom of the hourglass is the increase of My glory and power over My people.

Some of My Jonathans and Davids are old men and women now, but I say to you, Be like Caleb! Gird your sword on your thigh and go to war, fight and be strong in the power of My might, not your own. (Ephesians 6:10). Your age is irrelevant for I will pour out My Spirit upon all flesh including children, young people, middle aged and the elderly.

In your weakness you are strong. (2 Corinthians 12:9-10). I command you not to disqualify yourselves. David was a youth when he slew Goliath and Caleb was an old man when he fought the enemies of Israel. Your age and experience is nothing to me. I require you to have a humble and contrite heart, (Psalm 51:17) I require you to simply say, "Here I am. Send me." (Isaiah 6:8)

Finally I say to My Sauls, 'You need to prepare the Jonathans and Davids and be prepared to hand the keys over to them.' If you do this I will exceedingly reward you with honour and blessings. My Sauls, many of you have done well and run a good race, but you need to know that everything is about to change. You need to be brave and strong and when I instruct you, hand over the keys.

A new darkness is coming, a new enemy from the pit is being released, the old ways will no longer work or suffice. Only the warriors of faith will prevail against the unclean spirits that are coming. I love you My church, I love you all dearly. It's time to begin, it's time to dust off your swords, oil your shields, and put on the armour of God. It's time to go to war.

Christopher Wickland 27th of June 2023

I AM your song!

Isaiah 12:2 *'See! God is my salvation. I am confident and unafraid; for Yah ADONAI is my strength and my song, and he has become my salvation.'*

I AM your salvation. (Ps 62:1) I AM your exceedingly great reward. (Gen 15:1) I AM God almighty (Gen 17:1), who was, and is and is to come. (Rev 1:4) I AM love, (1 JN 4:16) and I love you with an everlasting love (Jer 31:3), a wonderful love which transcends all bounds of understanding. (Is 40:13-18)

If only My people knew how much I loved them, if only they grasped it. For perfect love casts out all fear (1 Jn 4:18) and knowing how much I love My people would set many free from their imperfections and fears. (Imperfections being aspects of the soul which is broken and damaged) (Lk 4:18)

I want My people to be confident in Me, (Eph 6:10-11) for I AM a God who will never fail or forsake you. (Deut 31:6) I never let My people down, even though many think I do. My people often perish through lack of knowledge and understanding (Hos 4:6). Some give up hope in Me, some even turn away from Me. My heart is always for My people, always has and always will be. (Mat 28:20; Jn 14:16-17; 2 Chr 7:16; 1 Cor 6:19)

I do not act and think as a man thinks (Num 23:19). My ways are higher, vast and eternal. (Is 55:8) I see and set the beginning from the end. (Is 46:10-11) I know that disappointments and heartaches often come to My people but I AM with you in the midst of your sadness. (Ps 34:19) I feel your pain also. Some things don't add up and make sense this side of eternity, yet across the veil all is clear. This is why you need to trust Me. (Prov 3:5-6) You need to be confident and unafraid My people. I AM trustworthy. (Deut 31:6)

I AM your strength, I AM your song, I AM your salvation. (Is 12:2) I want to encourage and comfort My people. I want My people to be blessed in knowing that I AM always with them and that I AM always trustworthy.

I AM your song, I AM your poetry, I AM your dance and joy. (John 15:10-11) As you grow in trust toward Me, I will give you new songs to sing, (Psalm 96:1) new poems to write, new pictures to draw and paint. I want to express Myself through you in beautiful and creative ways My people. (Ps 45:1; Ps 96:1; Ps 149:3)

Some of you have become monochrome and dull in your walk with Me. I do not wish you to see Me as dull or jaded. I AM creator God, (Neh 9:6) I set the colours in the rainbow, I put the beauty into the stars, I give the birds their morning and evening songs. (Ps 148:13; Job 12:7; Is 55:12) I AM a God of colour and your faith should reflect that.

Learn to dance again My people, learn to see the world in all its glorious colour. Rejoice in Me always and again I say rejoice. (Phil 4:4) The kingdom of God is righteousness, peace and joy. (Rom 14:17) I have poured out My Spirit of joy within you. (Is 61:3; Neh 8:10) I have filled you with the oil of gladness. (Is 61:3) Be creative in your worship, in your prayers and in your faith. (Eph 5:19) Be full of joy and colour, please don't be sad and grey.

Lift up your countenance upon Me, for My countenance is shining down upon you. (Num 6:26) See your life through My eyes of love toward you and not in the dullness of your own. Lean not on your own understanding but in all things trust Me. (Prov 3:5-6) For I AM your strength, your song and your salvation.

Chris Wickland 28th of June 2023

The days which are coming

Days are coming says the LORD where I will pour out terrible signs from the heavens. I shall hurl stars to the ground that will make the nations reel and stagger in shock.

I shall pour down fire from above that will scold and chastise the nations. These will be terrible signs that will make men weak at the knees and bring great consternation. There will be signs in the sun and moon, terrible signs that will fill the nations with fear. Many will try to explain these wonders away with science, but like the magicians of Egypt, there was a point where they were unable to do so.

The nations have come too far - I AM calling time on your technology, your finances and your Towers of Babel. I will hack you down and only leave a stump to remain. The watchers have decreed that man's great insolence and wickedness must be restrained before the Lawless One arises.

The nations will soon know that I AM GOD and that I AM King! Like the days of Sodom and Gomorrah I will pour down fire from heaven and scold and scorch nations with my wrath. The nations will know their place and they will be restrained for a season before the restraint is taken away to reveal the Lawless One.

I will pour out My Spirit on all flesh and I will call many back to Me in these days ahead. My people, you need to awake and arise from your slumber and sleep. I AM roused and rising up, the cry of the nations has come before Me and I must act accordingly.

Beware My saints that these signs that are coming will perplex and confuse many. For you will look to the scriptures and try to figure out that which has been sealed till the end of days.

These are not those days yet, but the climax that leads to the end of days. You are going to see signs that are both what you would call Old Testament and New Testament. I AM unchanging and I will do what I will do.

My people, My children you need to arise from your sleepy slumber. Be prepared for signs that will shock and awe. Blood and fire, hail and storm, signs in the heavens and down upon the earth. I will make the nations reel and stagger and all shall know that I AM God.

My people will learn to rightfully fear Me again and will learn to intercede again. My people are called to stay My hand but many are too asleep to know or to care.

Look to the heavens and watch, for the days of blood and fire are coming. My people will soon know that I AM their God. Pray and intercede for the nations for terrible signs are coming. Signs so profound that none will dare mock or explain them away. For I alone AM God. I ALONE AM KING.

Chris wickland 29th of June 2023

Adonai is mustering an army for war!

Isaiah 13:4. *'Listen! A tumult on the mountains - it sounds like a vast multitude! Listen! The uproar of kingdoms of the nations gathering together! ADONAI Tzva'ot is mustering an army for war.*

Firstly My saints, My glorious ones, learn to listen (Prov 4:20-22). I am not talking about your natural hearing but hearing spiritually (John 10:27; 8:47, 6:63). Listen! Can you hear it? Can you hear the sound on the mountains? Can you not hear the nations marching and conspiring against me? (Ps 2:1-3)

Surely they are marching and banging their drum of war. They want to dethrone Me, they want Me to be gone forever, they want to declare, 'There is no God.' (Ps 14:1) But I sit in the heavens and I laugh at them, I laugh them to scorn. (Ps 2:4) Foolish people, they see themselves as so great and they do not realise they are but dust, (Ps 103:13-14) they are so blind that they do not even know that they live and move and have their being because I allow it. (Acts 17:28) Foolish man, you are just like that old serpent you worship and follow. You think you are so great and wise and powerful, yet you are nothing more than a mere pawn to me. (Prov 19:21)

The nations think they finally have it, they believe they have Me and My people this time. How many past empires have failed who came against Me and My people? How many empires do I have to topple before man grasps with his mind that I alone am God?

But this time I have an army, a Gideon army. A seemingly small remnant army that in the natural amounts to nothing yet in the spiritual they are giants. (Judges 7:4-16). Fear not my remnant church, for the few that hold to Me and My truth may seem small in the realm of the natural. (Jer 42:2, Ezra 9:8, Is 1:9, Is 37:31-32) Fear not, wave your banners and standards, let the enemy see you standing and holding your ground. (Eph 6:13) Let them laugh, taunt and mock you because of your seeming weakness.

Your warfare my saints is not against flesh and blood but with powers of darkness in heavenly places. (Eph 6:12) Your weapons are not ones that cut and destroy flesh, no, your weapons are not carnal but they are spiritual for the tearing down of strongholds. (2 Cor 10:3-6)

As the nations assemble and advance, (Zech 12:3) My remnant army will fall to their knees, for there alone is the weapons of choice; prayer, humility and a contrite heart. (Ps 51:17) As the nations prepare for an easy victory I will suddenly come to the aid of Gideon. I will bend low the heavens and pour forth fire, blood and hail and come to the aid of My people. (Ps 144:5, Ps 18:9)

I will shake the nations, (Heb 12:27) I will do signs in the heavens above and on the earth below. (Acts 2:19) I will put arrogant man back in his place again. Then many shall see and turn from their wicked ways and join the army of Gideon. (2 Chron 7:14) In time the army of Gideon will become the army of David. It will be great in size and powerful being led by mighty men and women of God.

My people will learn that warfare is not won through carnal means. (Eph 6:12) No! My people will learn war is only ever won on the battlefield of prayer. Every victory, every advance to take the enemy's flag is only ever won through prayer.

My people, put aside your feeble notions, ideas and politics. Learn the true might of prayer, return to Me in prayer. Become a member of My army. Enlist today!

However, not everyone will want to do this, for many in that hour would rather trust in the wisdom of man and his programs than prayer.(1 Cor 2:5) Those who choose not to bend the knee in the days ahead will fall on the battlefield. (Prov 16:18) Those who bend the knee will be valiant on the battlefield. (1 Sam 17:45)

ADONAI Tzva'ot is mustering an army for war. Will you join the army of the LORD? Will you heed the call? Will you become My praying remnant and take your place with my angels? (2 Kings 6) Will you join Me on the battlefield to see My kingdom come? (Mat 6:10)

Chris Wickland. 3rd of July 2023

A taunt song to Stonewall

Isaiah 14:4-7. *'You will take up this taunt song against the king of Babel: "At last the oppressor is stilled, his arrogance ended! ADONAI has broken the staff of the wicked, the sceptre of the rulers, which furiously struck down peoples with unceasing blows. Angrily beating down nations with relentless persecution. The whole earth is at rest and quiet, they break into song."'*

I want to take up a taunt against you serpent, Stonewall. You who have perverted My ways on the land. Like a twisting serpent you writhe and put pressure on the neck of government. You hiss and whisper in the ears of power, you seduce many with your dark hypnotic eyes. You whisper that evil is good and good is evil. Oh Stonewall you seducing serpent, I taunt you with this song.

You have grown long and fat and have become arrogant thinking none can dethrone you from your serpent throne. You have become fat by what you devour, but I am going to cut off your supply of food. Indeed I am already doing it. Day by day you are losing influence, day by day losing power and you cannot even see it.

You sit like a dragon on a treasure of gold. Who would dare rouse you? Who would dare steal from you? You fat lazy serpent, I taunt you this day and will send my watchers who will take your gold from you. You fat lazy serpent, without your gold you hold no power over those in power. Without your gold you will become nothing but an unclean worm.

I have broken your staff, I have shattered your throne like glass, I have robbed you of your power, you thief, you usurper. I am removing your snake pit from the seat of power. I am robbing you of your power as you robbed others of theirs. For all power and authority is from Me and I will raise up and tear down as I see fit.

You foul serpent, seducing many to think you are beautiful, yet I see you for what you really are. I will lop off your head you old serpent, I will remove you from power and cast you out into the gutter.

Finally this land will be at rest and My people will rejoice in your downfall. Like the walls of Jericho, you will fall O serpent Stonewall. Your debris will be ground to powder, turned to dust, no more to be remembered, blown away on the winds of change.

Goodbye Stonewall, you have bruised my heal long enough and now I will crush your head and chop it off. From the pit you came and to the pit you shall return.

Chris Wickland 4th of July 2023

Jerusalem O Jerusalem

Ezekiel 7:11 *'Violence (Hamas) has grown into a rod of wickedness. None of them shall remain, nothing of their crowds, nothing of their wealth - there is nothing of importance in them.'*

Oh Israel, My daughter, My Zion. At this time you sit alone like a shelter in a vineyard. The nations gather round you and conspire against you. Acts of violence (Hamas) are brought against you from the sky and the airwaves.

When you suffer, you sit alone in silent patience with no one to help you, none to defend your cause. Yet I AM your ADONAI, I AM merciful and I will not reject you O My people. I take no pleasure in causing you grief or pain. I AM your shield and your very great reward.

I know Israel, that you have become tired, you have become weary. You have become as one who walks around the same mountain year on year. 'Pray for the peace of Jerusalem!' Yet Shalom seems to evade the city of peace. Like an old garment, you have become tired and stretched thin.

Let Me comfort you O Jerusalem, for you are the city of Ariel. I will bring back that which is lost to you, that which your heart desires everyday. I will return that which I took from you My people. I will give you back your heart, that you may stand strong until the end.

In this hour I want to show favour and compassion to you. The enemy has come like a flood to you, but I will raise up My standard against violence (Hamas) in these days. You will no longer sit as a shack in a field of cucumbers. (Isaiah 1:8)

Watch My people, I will raise up nations who will stand up for you, who will defend your cause. I will even cause some who are your enemies to be your allies in the days ahead.

I will raise up sheep nations that will stand alongside you My Ariel. The land of three Lions will come to your aid soon with strength and military power. When they do, you will stand shoulder to shoulder with others whom I will raise to shield you from violence (Hamas).

You are My suffering servant and much pain lies ahead, but the days of Peace from the city of Peace are coming, when I shall rule and reign as your ADONAI from Mount Zion and my glory shall cover the earth as the waters.

Chris Wickland 5th of July 2023

Get ready to enter the promised land

Deuteronomy 1:6 & 8 *'The LORD our God spoke to us in Horeb saying, 'You have stayed long enough on this mountain. Look, I have set the land before you: Go in! Possess the land which the LORD swore to your fathers, Abraham, Isaac, and Jacob, to give to them and their seed after them.'*

My people you have stayed long enough in this wilderness, in this dry and arid land. A wilderness that is harsh and barren, where things are difficult to grow and prosper. I signal the shofar (trumpet) blast. It's time for the people of God to move out of the wilderness into a land that is flowing with milk and honey.

The great exodus must now begin. Pack up your things and prepare to advance for all that you have known for the last 40 years is over. My people, the wilderness has been hard on you and you have diminished in number, yet what the enemy has taken I will require back a hundred fold. For every one lost I will claim back a hundred from the enemy. That which came to do harm and damage will turn into blessing and life.

Rise up My people and finally get ready to advance into the promised land of revival. Possess the land that I have sworn to you through your fathers in this land. For the vision is yet for an appointed time, but at the end it shall speak, and not lie: though it tarry, wait for it; because it will surely come, it will not tarry. (Hab 2:3). I am not a man that I should lie. (Num 23:19). So My word that comes from My mouth will not return to me void, but it will accomplish that which I please and it shall prosper in what I send it to do. (Is 55:11). For I watch over My word to perform it. (Jer 1:12). That which I have promised shall be revealed and you shall see My goodness on the land of the living. (Ps 27:13)

But be warned My people, this will be no easy journey or occupation. Taking the land of your inheritance will be severely resisted by the enemy. He does not want you taking back the ground he has worked so hard to claim for his own. He will throw all his weapons at you, fear, discouragement, and hopelessness. You must keep your eyes fixed on Me. Do not look at the storms which will rage violently to your left and to your right.

Taking this land will not be by might, nor by power, nor by the programs of man, but by My Spirit. (Zec 4:6)   Do not carry my ark (presence of God) in an unworthy manner or you will suffer the fate of Uzzah. I do not want My ark touched by the hands of men seeking their own glory and their own name.   Things must be done accordingly, for the ways of the Spirit will transcend the carnal thinking mind.

I will raise up my Joshuas', Moses', Miriams' and Deborahs', in the days to come. They are anointed ones to lead my people to victory in taking the land. Man will not self appoint himself any more for I will not allow it. I will not allow Uzzah to touch My ark.   I will raise up and I will raise low in these days.

Put on your full armour of God, be strong in Me and in the power of My might. (Eph 6:10-18) Gird your loins for action, (1 Pet 1:13) work with one hand and have the other holding the sword of the Spirit. (Neh 4:17). Get ready to fight and work.   Fight the enemy, stand your ground, submit to Me and he will flee like a coward. (Eph 6:13, James 4:7). Labour in building My church and restore the broken ruins.

These will be difficult yet glorious days. The work and warfare will be hard for you. For the harvest is great and the workers are few. (Mat 9:37). The burden for souls will be great, yet My burden is light. Carry My burden and not your own. (Mat 11:28-30) All those who are faithful and fight and build my temple in the days ahead will all be remembered, their names will be written in the archives of heaven. Not one single dot or tittle will be forgotten and I will reward you for your sacrifice and your service.

The shofar (trumpet) is sounding. It's now time to arise, pack your things and get ready to take the land.

Chris Wickland 10th of July 2023

The rending of the cloth

Ezekiel 9:4. *'And the LORD said to him (the angel), Go through the midst of the city, through the midst of Jerusalem, and set a mark upon the foreheads of the people who sigh and who cry over all the abominations that are done in its midst.'*

My dear saints, the ones who have chosen not to defile their garments (Rev 3:4) with the stains of worldliness, I want to encourage you with these words. Many of you have a heavy heart due to the abominations being practised in My church, My body. (Ez 9:4)

Many who claim to hold to My Name have bent the knee to the spirit of the world and have embraced it and all its harlotries. This will not be permitted for much longer; I will not have My house profaned with abominations. (Ezk 8) My house is supposed to be a house of prayer so that I may pour out blessings and healing upon your land. (Is 56:7, 2 Chr 7:14)

I will bring a rending of the cloth, it will be torn top to bottom. (1 Sam 15:27-29) I will separate the clean garment from the soiled, the pure in heart, from the profane and adulterous. My people do not be surprised when you see the church of this land become split. The defiled will be taken from that which is clean. I will separate the wheat from the chaff, the goats from the sheep. (Lk 3:13, Mat 25:31-46)

I will not allow my holy ones to endure any more corruption, (Ps 125:3) for I am a jealous God (Ex 20:3, 34:14) and I will separate them out for myself. (1 Pet 2:9) Indeed all those who are sad and groan at the state of the church in this nation have been marked and noted. (Ez 9:4) They will be set apart for Me, and they will be rewarded by Me for not bending the knee to Baal.

My altars have been defiled and profaned, (Mal 1:7, Ez 43:8) my wine (blood) and bread (body) given to those who should never have it. (Ex 12:43-47) For how can light and darkness coexist? How can I stand with Belial? So, because of this, for the sake of My own who will not bow the knee, I will reward you and separate you from them.

Some of you will be removed to safety, some of you will stay and see the rebellious torn away from you. I have allowed the wheat and tares to come to full term and My sickle is raised to harvest. I will separate out truth from error, wheat from chaff and sheep from goats. (Mat 13:24-43, 25:31-46)

Do not be surprised when you see this, do not wonder where I am in the chaos. You must simply trust and obey Me and hold tight to Me and Me alone. I AM your *'Shaddai'* (Gen 17:1-8) and your exceedingly great reward. (Gen 15:1) Remember not all in the church are in MY church. The chaff must fall away and leave for the new thing which I am about to release in this nation (UK).

I will sow together all those who have not soiled their garments and bring together My church in a way that is as radical as the reformation was in its day. The old reformation was a separating, but the reformation that is coming is a re-forming of that which has been lost. My church will no longer schism and sub-divide, rather I will reform them together in a new unity of Spirit.

Stand tall and strong My people, for My angels are coming to separate the wheat from the chaff. (Mat 13:24-43)

Chris Wickland 11th of July 2023

The Stained Glass Window

Ezekiel 11:19 *'And I will give them One heart and I will put a new spirit within you and will give them a heart of flesh.'*

I will give My people one heart soon. A heart that is My heart. A heart that my true church will beat with, where all my people beat with one heart to the same beat.

My people are broken and schismed and this is not healthy. In this there can never be any kind of true unity.

Birds of a feather often flock together. However I am doing a new thing, a wonderful thing where birds of a feather will not flock together. No. They will be a menagerie of different flocks and different breeds.

Many will ask how such a thing can be? It is because I will give them one new heart. They are all different yet they all share the same heart.

Man's way is to stick to one's own kind. This is not my way. I respect the different breeds of my people but I don't want them singled out according to kind. I want them to be one in heart not in kind or breed.

My prayer is that that My church be one. It began as one and has now become broken like glass. Shards all over the floor with no possibility of repair.

However, I am going to take this broken glass and form a stained glass work of art from the fragments. I am not going to fix the brokenness. No, rather I am going to piece the brokenness of the coloured glass to create a single piece of artwork. The beauty of this stained glass window will be in the colours of the broken shards.

I will take those broken pieces and put them together into something new. Then with the light of my Son shining through, all will gaze and marvel upon this new but old church. A church that is truly one, not by uniformity but in unity of heart and purpose.

Chris Wickland 13th of July 2023

The changing of the guard

Isaiah 57:1-2 *'The righteous perish, and no man lays it to heart and men of loving kindness are taken away, no one considering that the righteous one is taken away from the evil to come. He will enter into peace: they will rest in their beds, each one walking in his uprightness.'*

Many righteous saints have passed of late and not many of My people are taking it to heart. They are not pondering and meditating upon this sign, for surely the righteous should live and not die. (Ez 33:13) So why are they dying? Have you not considered or wondered why?

A new season has now come upon the earth and a veil of darkness is creeping over the nations. The old previous season has now closed and thus many generals of the guard have and are being taken home. They have run the race, they have finished their travail upon the earth. They are My good and faithful servants and its time for them to enter into their reward. (Mat 25:21)

Yet, would I leave My church without fathers, (1 Jn 2:14) mothers and generals of faith? No, of course not! I love My people with a tender love and My heart is always for My people. I will raise up new apostles, prophets, evangelists, pastors and teachers for this season. (Eph 4:11) Some of these leaders will seem to be as ones abnormally born. (1 Cor 15:8) They will suddenly emerge from nowhere and grow in prominence quickly. Mark and note these people, for many of them shall be the leaders who will help march many of My people to the frontlines of the coming Great War.

But some are saying in the camp, 'No, there will not be leaders or superstars in the coming move of God.' Yet this is what I say, 'Check your heart My people, for your hearts are transparent before Me and no lie is hid from before My gaze. (Heb 4:13) I have compassion on My people and they must have shepherds to lead them. (Mat 9:36) You are right in that you say there will be no superstars, this is true from the worldly perspective. However, there will be spiritual giants in the days coming, the days of Noah.(Mat 24:37) These will be My giants that will walk the earth, mighty men and women of God who have given everything to follow Me and accept the great and costly calling I have placed upon them. It is these generals who will lead My people to the front lines of the Great War in the Valley of Decision under the blood red sky. (Joel 3:14, Rev 6:12)

Do not fear the coming darkness My people, do not let it concern you in your pursuit of Me and My will. How can My stars shine if there is no darkness to shine in. It is Me who is allowing the darkness to increase, so that My stars may shine brightly to be a witness in the days ahead. Look up to your natural sky and behold the wonder of it. The darker the sky the more stars are seen. My righteous ones will shine like stars. (Dan 12:3).

As Israel grew and became like the stars in the heavens for number, (Gen 26:4) so will My church in these days. Do not fear the darkness My people, for in the darkness My light will shine and many will come out of the shadow of darkness into My light in the coming days. (Is 9:2)

So ponder the death of My righteous ones, they have finished their race and it's time for them to be rewarded. (Is 57:1-2) Note, this as a sign from Me to you My people. The season has changed, autumn has now cast its shadow upon the earth. It is time to change the guard. My servant Moses was not allowed to lead My people into the promised land. He took Israel as far as I permitted him to go and then I brought Him home to Me. It took Joshua, a military leader to take the people the next step of the journey. The same is true now. Moses My servant is dead! (Josh 1:2)

I declare a new guard to lead My people in these days, a new guard who will in time become church fathers and mothers who will lead My church to hand over the baton to the last generation to face the Great War in the Valley of Decision under the blood red sky.

Christopher Wickland 17th of July 2023

Oh My Church of England
Based on Ezekiel chapter 16

Church of England, I remember the day you were born. You were born from blood, heartache and treachery. You were despised by many at your birth, even in this green and pleasant land. Yet I saw you in your infancy, in your nativity and I took compassion upon you. And when I passed by you and saw you in your blood of birth I said, 'Live! Yes I said to you in your blood, 'Live!'

I caused you to multiply and grow in strength, in honour and dignity. You grew in stature before Me, you became beautiful and regal in this land. A beautiful Amethyst set in green clover. You were Mine and I was yours. Through you this land was blessed, this land was safe, I was pleased to call you My church. You excelled in your beauty and became the honour of kings, queens and the mighty.

I clothed you with embroidered work and dressed you with fine linen and covered you with silk. I decked you with ornaments and I put bracelets upon your hands and a chain upon your neck. I gave to you the privilege of anointing kings and queens. I bequeathed to you great honour, riches and prestige.

However, in time you trusted in your own beauty and strength. You became proud and pompous and slowly but surely you turned your back on Me. You played the harlot because of your renown. You took the gold, the silver and the jewels I gave you and made for yourself images of men and did commit harlotry. You have set my oil, incense, flesh and blood before a profane altar. You have abandoned Me in pursuit of your own glory instead of promoting Mine.

I have heard your profane prayers, I have seen your abominations and wickedness. You have forsaken Me in your pursuit to hunt down power, influence and lovers. I have to call you what you are, you have become a harlot before Me.

However, there are many who have not defiled and soiled their garments within you, there are many who grieve over you. There are many who have cried, travailed and prayed to Me on your behalf. To those who have remained faithful to Me I say this, 'Because of you and your intercessions, I will relent from a full chastisement to the Church of England.' You will see some painful days coming as My chastisement is worked out. I will half her strength and greatly humble her. She will lose her position of honour for a season.

I will leave a remnant, those who love Me, who will not leave her but endure her pains as their own. I will leave her as a stump, but in time she will return to Me and fresh branches will grow and she will again increase in might. I will then turn to her and restore her and will love her again and be pleased to call her My church.

For thus says Adonai, the LORD, I shall deal with you as you have done, you who have despised the oath you took before Me. Nevertheless I shall remember the oath sworn by those previous and I will remember you and look kindly upon you as I did at your nativity. I will remain faithful to those who have remained faithful to Me.

Finally to My faithful, be strong, be courageous and endure the chastisement, set your faces like flint and look for the joy set before you. You will see the harlot become true again and I promise to restore her and be pleased to call her My own in the days ahead.

Chris Wickland. 18th of July 2023

The tide and waves of My Spirit

1 Corinthians 15:46. *'The spiritual did not come first, but the natural, and after that the spiritual.'*

As you ponder the natural world, I want you to ponder upon its spiritual lesson. You can discern the sky but why can you not discern the signs of the times? (Mat 16:3)

Are you not supposed to be an Issachar generation? Do you not have the mind of Christ? (1 Chron 12:32. Rom 13:11-14, 1 Cor 2:16)

Why is it that I gave you ears, yet you neither hear nor listen? Why is it that I gave you eyes, yet you neither see nor perceive. Are you so dull of heart My people that you do not yet understand the meaning of the leaven of the Pharisees?

When I speak to you of spiritual things you think I am talking about the natural and when I talk about the natural you think I am talking about the spiritual.

So I say to you My people, 'Look at the shore line, what do you see? Can you see the waves and the tides that drive them? Do you see waves with your eyes, or can you see My parables hidden within them? In hearing can you hear, in seeing can you see? Are your hearts so dull that you cannot hear and see what the Spirit is saying to the churches?

The tide is coming in, but it is coming in on waves. Sometimes those tidal waves are strong whilst others are weak. The tide has been out for some time but the tide has now turned. This is no ordinary tide that is coming, no, it is a storm surge. This tide will come quickly and I will raise the water level against this land.

These waves will bring both devastation and great blessing. For those who have built their lives on Me and My teachings, the waves will bless you. For those who have built their lives upon the shifting sands of the vain philosophies of man, they will surely fall and great will be their fall.

Two tides are to be expected. The first is a storm surge, this will drive the filth from off this land (UK). These waters will rip through everything which claims to be of Me. Those that are true will remain, that which is false or not right will fall. Expect to see many ministries, organisations and churches which claim to be of Me vanish. Remember judgement starts with the house of God. (1 Pet 4:17)

The first tide will come with great stormy winds that will be known as the 'winds of change.' They will blow across this land, even through the hearts of My people; be prepared to be tested. Are you for Me or are you really against Me? The Wind will check your hearts and that which motivates you.

After the storm surge and purging, I will quickly send another tide, this will be a tide of great blessing. It will bring new life wherever it goes. This will be known as the 'Great Wave of Revival!'

Those that remain standing after the first tide will be blessed by the second tide. Those who fell in the first tide can have little to no part in the second tide. I will bless those who stand for Me and whose hearts have been tested by the 'winds of change.'

Equinox, Equinox, Equinox, the Spirit says. Learn from this to see what's coming both in the Spirit and in the natural.

My people, get ready to brace yourself, for the storm surge is coming. Hold tight to Me, for I alone am your Ark. Please endure the storm and set your faces like flint and look toward the joy of the second tide that quickly follows.

I AM coming soon, I AM moving in waves. Can you see, can you hear what the Spirit is saying to the churches?

Christopher Wickland 20th of July 2023

My knights of the round table

The Round Table concept is that all who sit at the table are equal. There is no fighting over status, rank and ego. There is no head at the Round Table. The Round Table represents chivalry in its highest form. The knights of the Round Table pledge loyalty to Jesus and His church. The Round Table symbolises equality, unity and oneness.

Psalm 133:1 & 3. '*How good and pleasant it is when brothers live together in harmony…For there the LORD bestows His blessing, even life forevermore.*'

A popular concept that is being proposed in these days is that of the Round Table. The notion of the fivefold ministry coming together to sit at the table and share the heart of God from the different aspects of the fivefold, to enable a full counsel of God's heart and will to His church.

This is a concept that sadly very few will attempt and it will be men and women of brave hearts who will try to attempt this. Yet this is something I feel the Spirit of God is encouraging and wanting to be pursued in the days ahead. These Round Tables are about gleaning a fuller picture of what God is doing, and saying to His church nationally, regionally and locally.

I feel there needs to be both local, regional and national Round Tables so that the counsel of God can be assessed for the local, the regional and the national points of view. What God may be saying nationally may need to be looked and processed from a regional and then local point of view. ie Local churches can work together in implementing elements of God's heart for the nation in the local area. This also works the other way around but to a lesser degree, from the local to the regional and in some cases, to the national. This fulfils the basic parameters set out in Exodus 18:17-26.

There will need to be an integrity of those who sit at the table if this is to work. Churches will not listen to the singular voice of the Round

Table if there is no integrity and accountability. Self appointed leaders with no accountability to others will not engender trust of any kind. There can be no lone wolves or unaccountable shepherds and prophets. Therefore one who sits at a Round Table locally, regionally or national must therefore be blameless in respect to their life in God. They must be sensible, respectable and teachable. They must not be violent, argumentative, unteachable, unaccountable and a lover of money. They must be thought well of by others and not given over to pride. They must be genuine people/leaders and not two faced or hypocritical. They must have a proven track record in their 5 fold field of ministry. They must be seen to be walking in their relevant ministries and recognised as such locally, regionally and nationally; depending on which Round Table they will sit on.

It goes without saying that all five fold ministries must be present at the table. This is true for national and regional. However, it may be that only 3 or 4 ministries of the 5 fold be represented in a small local area. In this case they must work in the context in which they find themselves. ie, a round table of 3 ministries but working with the regional table that represents 5.

The conversations of the round tables must be open for all churches to hear. This may be done via emails, published papers, web pages and social media. It is then up to the regional and local churches if they want to implement changes or not.

There must always be choice from the counsel of Round Tables. Thus no control, no manipulation and no hierarchy to regional and local churches. It is up to the local churches wether they listen, adhere or ignore the Round Tables. This will engender trust, partnership and commonality.

Round Tables, locally, regionally and nationally must be forged through friendship and fellowship. This may not always prove easy but Jesus chose very different people to become His twelve apostles, the very foundations of the Church.

The five fold ministries represented must also be across the denominational divide where possible, ie Protestant, Catholic and Orthodox.

Round Tables don't need to be represented by an individual although it can. Round Tables can also have groups, ie groups of evangelists, prophets, pastors etc as well as singular prophets, pastors, apostles etc.

Round Tables are not a 'Churches Together' event. Rather it is a specific coming together to seek the Lord for His heart within His church, His mission, His leading and direction for the church internationally, nationally, regionally and locally.

At the Round Tables no one ministry is greater or lesser than another. ie, apostolic doesn't trump the pastoral etc. At the Round Table all are equal and have the same amount of say as the next.

The Round Table should also be a place where difficult issues can be discussed and resolved, ie church councils like in Acts chapter 15.

The Round Table is not a place for politicking and winning votes, for all are equal at the table. The table should speak with one voice to the church, but a singular voice that speaks from the many voices of the five fold.

Round Tables of similar ministries is not advisable, ie, a table of just prophets or evangelists. The Round Table is a symbol of unity across the diversity of the five fold ministries. However councils of individual ministries I think would be most welcome and valuable.

How does this all begin? It starts as a movement, where like-minded Christians who recognise the need for such a thing start to come together to potentially form Round Tables. In time the movement builds momentum and relationship with other Round Tables. It then becomes a Nexus and slowly but surely connects to other Round Tables around the country, again through friendship, trust and community.

Finally we should be careful to not get sidetracked with Arthurian legends and fables about the Round Table. The Table is merely a symbol and principle. Let's not make this something that it is not and cause it to lose credibility before it even starts.

Chris Wickland 24th of July 2023.

My Remnant

Zechariah 13:8-9 *'And it will be in all the land, says the LORD, two parts there will be cut off and die, but the third will be left there. And I shall bring the third part through the fire and will refine them as silver is refined and will try them as gold is tried. They will call on My name and I will hear them. I will say, it is My people; and they will say, "The LORD is my shepherd.'*

My people, My people, I love My people, My church, My bride in waiting. I have such a tender love toward you and my heart aches with longing for you. I speak to those who have remained faithful and have not capitulated to the vain philosophies of man. You are My beautiful and precious remnant. I want to encourage you with these words, My faithful saints.

Firstly, well done for standing firm to the truths of My word and holding to the teachings of My gospel. Well done for not calling sin good and good sin. I want to comfort your troubled hearts.

Over the years you have seen many turn away from Me, some suddenly, others over time. It has broken your heart to see the state of My people in this nation. For this I will greatly reward you, you will be forever remembered in heaven for standing firm for My name in these days.

My Remnant, times of testing are now coming and I don't want you to get caught up in My judgements upon this nation. Come out of her My people, do not associate yourselves with the sins of this nation. Come aside and make your garments white and clean before Me. I need to remind you that judgement starts with the house of God and so in this hour of testing stand strong in your faith. As the great shaking comes to this nation, stand strong, stand tall and endure it. The great shaking will bring many gods and idols crashing down but do not fear. Allow this time of judgement on this nation to be a time of refining for you.

Humble yourselves under the mighty hand of God, allow Me to refine, test and purge you. Let your metal be tested, let your metal be strong and true. Do not fear or resist the testing of your metal, rather endure it with endurance and fortitude, for your reward will be great.

I wish to make you Christ-like, I wish to make you stronger than you have ever been before. You are still not ready to be used in the ways I wish to use you just yet but in time you will be ready. You will be purged, refined and made strong through the fires of circumstance and trial. All that can be shaken will be shaken, the testing of your hearts will produce pure gold. A gold I can use to adorn My temple, My church in the days ahead. I promise you that the glory of this latter temple will be superior and more glorious than the current and former.

In that day, you shall call upon Me and I will hear all your prayers and answer them. You shall see Me move in remarkable and lovely ways, you will see My kindness and tenderness and you shall know that I AM the LORD, The Good Shepherd; for you are My people and I AM your God.

Christopher Wickland 25th of July 2023

My prodigals shall return

Luke 15:14,17-18. '..*After he had spent everything freely, a severe famine came throughout that country, and he began to be lacking. And then he came to himself and said, 'How many hired hands of my father abound in food, but I am dying here in the famine. When I get up I shall go to my father and say to him, 'Father, I have sinned against heaven and before you...'.*

I want to encourage My people with these comforting words, "The prodigals will be coming home very soon." My heart yearns and groans for my children to come back home to Me. So many have left My vineyard and have wondered into waterless places. There are so many that have left me and have gone into the world and to the world around they seem totally lost to Me. Yet many still carry the spark of life in their tormented spirits.

I am about to blow my trumpet of chastisement upon the UK. I am calling time on your pride O Britannia. I will shake your financial institutions to breaking, I will shake your house of parliament to collapse in rubble, I will shake your churches that claim to be of Me yet are not. However, in this terrible famine that is coming, I will cause so many of my prodigals to wake up to their senses.

My prodigals will realise that without Me they truly have nothing and will die, they will see the folly of their ways. They will turn from their blindness and madness and will come before Me on bended knee and say, '*Father, I have sinned against heaven and before you.*' In their repentance I will hold out My loving arms to them and hug them and weep over them and heal them. I will heal their hurts, wounds and brokenness which caused them to leave My vineyard in the first place. I will bind up their sicknesses, I will heal their afflictions. For I AM The Lord that healeth thee.

In My chastisement which is about to blow through this land, note My grace which swiftly follows the repentant. In a time of great upheaval and shaking you will also see Me moving wonderfully. I am calling My own back. That which the devil stole will become mine again.

Many of those who return will become strong voices against the lies and deceptions of this hour. They will be my heralds and champions against the depravity of the day. Mark My words, satan will wish he never had tempted and tested them. Those he stole to become his trophies, will become My champions and will thrust the word of truth against his ruthless and wicked lies.

You have no idea just how many prodigals are coming home, you have no idea at all. You will be stunned and in shock when you see them coming and Oh there is so many of them coming home, so, so many.

Christopher Wickland 31st of July 2023

My people are asleep

Luke 22:46. *'And Jesus said to them, "Why are you sleeping? After you get up you must pray persistently, so that you would not enter a trial.'*

'Wake up o sleeper, rise up from the dead and Christ will shine on you.' (Eph 5:14)

New Atheism has taken over our nation and with it all the barriers and borders of morality have gone out of the window. When we say there is no God, we open the doors for madness. Everything is up for reinterpretation, deconstructionism and truth becomes as subjective and paradoxical as Schrodinger's Cat.

The church throughout history has stood up for the concept that man is made in the image of God, the 'Imago Dei.' Man is not random star dust caused from a hypothetical Big Bang. Rather, he is an extremely intricate created being made after the very likeness of God and thus must be treated as such. Yet now, thanks to the wonders of atheistic humanism, we now offer boil in the bag funerals where our late loved ones can now be boiled and reduced to compost because it's good for the environment.

Our culture has become far removed from Rene Descartes's philosophy of, 'I think, therefore I am.' Which is based on the notion that one could not doubt their own existence. However, today we have now drifted into notions of madness, 'I think I am a cat, therefore I am a cat.'

What concerns me during these days is the churches lack of direction and voice on the crisis that is happening to our society. We are asleep at the wheel. We should be awake and speaking into the issues of the signs of the times but instead we would rather be woke. We should be speaking truth to power yet the church has become almost silent on the issues of the day.

Wilberforce and others spoke into the wickedness of slavery. William and Catherine Booth took on the government regarding child labour laws. Today we have Christian Concern fighting the Goliaths of our day, whilst the church sits still and even criticises those who fight against the injustices of 'wokery.' The church in her silence has become complicit in compounding the errors and destructions that have come through the woke ideologies of today.

Saint Augustine called the church the 'City of God.' It is supposed to be a place where the culture of the kingdom of God comes out into the world around. However, some churches sit on the intersection of the sewers of man's muck and philosophies. The church instead of influencing culture has sadly become a septic tank filled with the influences of the world. The church is supposed to expose the deeds of darkness, not be complicit with it.

Has God spoken to His church and told her to be silent on the issues of our day? Has God commanded His church to be asleep, to batten down the hatches and hope this will all just go away? In the garden of Gethsemane Jesus asked the question, 'Why are you asleep?' Of all the times the disciples shouldn't be asleep was at the most crucial point in Jesus' life. He needed His people to pray, He needed His people to be alert and aware that the hour of the authority of darkness had come upon them. (Lk 22:53)

We are at a crossroads in this nation. We have a crisis of faith, of spiritual and mental health, of identity, of government and possible financial upheavals down the road. We have not seen a societal existential revolution of this magnitude since the reformation. The sexual revolution of the sixties looks more like a picnic in the park compared to that of today. We are driving headlong into the unknown with no breaks and no headlights.

The church is not listening to the prophetic clarion call, she is even refusing to see the world around and its complexities and problems. The church which is to be an Issachar voice is simply refusing to note the signs of the times. The bible tells the church to watch for the signs of the times and to watch and pray. (Mat 16:3, 26:41)

The church has become weak and lethargic and the world is watching us closely. It is as though the body of Christ no longer wants the hassle of speaking the truth. She is in a place of petrification. She fears the world more than she fears the Word. Did not Jesus learn obedience through suffering? (Heb 5:8). Did He ever shrink away from the powers of the day when He walked the earth?

Surely we must understand that there is a cost to pay to speak truth to power? Did we not consider that being a disciple requires us to lay down our lives for Jesus and suffer for Him, to be persecuted and marginalised for Him? Did Jesus not warn us about this? (John 15:20). So let us reason together, (Is 1:18) Why are we not speaking truth, why are we refusing to shine in days of such darkness? Surely God will require a reckoning of us.

Are we to be found wanting? In days where we should be praying, we are at ease. 'Woe to those at ease in Zion, you push away every thought of coming disaster, yet your actions only bring the day of judgement closer. You recline at table and feast and are merry, you sing your songs and fancy yourselves as so great, you care nothing about the ruin of your nation.' (Amos 6:1-6 Excerpts). Those words of Amos should ring sharply in our ears for these days.

Do we really want to be held accountable for the sins of our nation? For surely God will if we do not wake up. The church needs to be standing in the gap to stay God's hand. We are busy about our daily tasks when we should be about our Father's business. These words which I am writing are serious words, for we are not taking God's word seriously. We are not standing in the gap for this nation in our prayers and with our voices.

The scriptures teach us that if we do not stand in the gap for our nation then He will pour out His judgement upon our nation and He will hold us accountable for the judgement brought. (Ez 22:30, 33:1-6). Will God not present this judgement at our feet? Is this what we want?

I believe a time of trial and testing is coming to this nation but God does not want His people to be caught unawares. He wants His people to be spared this trial. Yet, the crucible of fire is often where the church goes. There in the fire, God removes the dross and imperfections. There God brings us back to our first love.

God needs His people to pray, to stay His hand. We need to stand in the gap for our nation. For the sake of ten righteous God would not destroy that ancient city, how much more can the church today stay His hand from a severe chastisement?

2 Chronicles 7:14. 'If My people who are called by My name, shall humble themselves and pray and seek My face and turn from their wicked ways, then will I hear from heaven and I will forgive their sin and will heal their land.'

Christopher Wickland 8th of August 2023

Dream of the shakings to come

The date is 13/08/23 and in the night hours I had a dream which I believe is from the Lord. Please weigh and test as you see fit.

The dream was relatively brief, yet it left me awake all night in prayer for our nation and the church of the UK. The dream began with me being inside a lady's house. The house itself was large with a sizeable back garden with a hedge of protection all the way about. Inside the front room of the house was many windows and a glass door which people entered and left from.

Suddenly the ground shook violently as an earthquake ripped through the nation. Things in the house began to fall as the ground rocked too and fro. No sooner had the shaking stopped that the sky lit up with an enormous flash of light. In the dream it was already day light and the flash was three times brighter than the day. I knew that the shaking was to do with the economy, the government and the church being shaken with judgement and chastisement. I also recognised immediately that the flash in the sky was nuclear and that Russia had done something really bad.

I knew from here on in we were in trouble and I felt the fear from people wanting to get into the house because we were considered a safe place. I must be honest, this seemed strange to me in a house with single glazed windows and a simple glass door. The house didn't seem safe in the natural, yet it was deemed to be so by outsiders. The woman of the house wanted to let people in, yet I hid down because I didn't want people to see us and was worried that we could be opening the doors to any crazy person who could do great harm to us. However, the woman of the house insisted on letting people in. Then in anger I opened the front door and proclaimed that all who wanted to enter into this house must first go and get every can of food, every bar of soap and every box of washing powder they could get from their household before they could come into the safety of the house. This seemed to me a very difficult request, especially because of the nature of the uncertainty and danger of outside. Yet people did what I demanded, much to my surprise.

In the next part of the dream the people living in the house who brought all their goods had access to limited rations of food, washing powder etc as they needed it but on a strict allotment process. I saw what looked like supermarket shelves full of food, washing powder etc. Through everyone bringing in their resources it helped everyone within the house to live in a place of relative safety and limited comfort.

I think the dream is quite clear in what it is portraying. The house and the woman owner represents the church. The people trying to get in is the people of the world wanting to come into the safety of the church. The earthquake represents the judgement and chastisements to the nation in our economy, the government and the church.
The nuclear flash represents the breaking out of what leads into World War 3. The practical storage and distribution of food is similar to the principle of Joseph in the book of Genesis who stored grain to help feed both the Israelites and the Egyptians through a terrible famine.

Many Christians are often distraught at the sight of Rainbow flags and banners being used in what they would see as derogatory. Yet these are prophetic signs of the day, for it will be just as in the days of Noah. The sins and wickedness that we have allowed on our country and in the nations will require a deluge to destroy it. This deluge, this tidal wave or Tsunami will be, I believe, God's chastisement upon us for allowing these things.

Yet amidst this great darkness that is to come will also come a wonderful tender move of God. The revival we have so longed for will come but not how we thought. For it will be the best of times and the worst of times.

As many of you know, I have been talking about these things coming for some time now and some may rightly be asking, 'When is all this going to happen?' Honestly, I do not know. I believe that the economic shakings have begun and will continue to worsen over the next couple of years until the system breaks.

Importantly though, I do not consider myself as a self styled prophet. I am really just a Pastor of a couple of small churches in a town no-one has heard of. I have a prophetic edge and share this often but that is all I am. These words will either come true or they will not. I literally will stand or fall on these messages I have been giving over the last 5 years or so. If I am wrong, then I will be hung out to dry by many people.

So we all have to pray, for either God is speaking or He is not. If He is not then I am deemed a false messenger and that's the end of me and my ministry. But if God is speaking, then what should our response be and how are we going to react and treat the voice of God? Also, if it is the voice of God, how much is from man and how much is from the Lord? The body needs to pray and discern in this hour, for the sands of time are running out and a reckoning is coming.

I will leave this with you, and you can consider or discard as you see fit.

God bless.

Christopher Wickland 13th of August 2023

The enemy's plans will backfire

This is a prophecy I received the day before I died. I found it on my phone several months later and released it. This was before lockdown started.

28 November 2019, Pastor Chris, of Living Word Church Network had received this prophecy. After recovering from the near-fatal cardiac arrest, he finally published it on 10 April, writing on Facebook: "I knew when I received this word the enemy was angry. The plan of the enemy is to shut every church down. No more prayer, no warfare of praise, no glory to God."

He added: "After chastisement, God will make the Church grow exponentially. The very weapon Satan used to destroy the Church will be the very thing that causes the Church to explode in growth."

"I will have the people in this land in derision", says the Lord. "I will pour out my Spirit on this land and those people that have called to come together to conspire, to tear down My ways and My precepts and My ordinances from this land – this green and pleasant land. Mark My words: I will have them in derision. I am in the heavens and I laugh at their futility, at the things that they're attempting to do, to close Me off and shut Me off from My own creation and so close down and shut down My people. For that is their ultimate aim. They want Me and every trace of Me eradicated from the land and from education and from every part of this society.

"But mark My words; I have plans to prosper this country, and I will bring to shame the wise. I will shame those who have so loftily held their heads up – their stiff-necked heads that have said, 'We will bring our ways! We will bring in our precepts and ordinances in this land, and we will eradicate God, and we will take Him off his throne. And we shall destroy His church.' But not so!

"Sadly, My own Church has failed to see how impoverished and how weakened she has become. She is literally now a remnant in this country. Yet I will do great things with a remnant. Yet I can take three hundred foot-soldiers with Gideon and do a great deliverance and I will do the same also in this land. I will take this small remnant of a

Church that is left, those Christians that genuinely acknowledge Me as their Lord and Saviour and will not bow the knee to Baal and to all his false practices and customs in respect to the laws that are now passing in this land.

"Mark My words, punishment will come for the sins that have covered this land. But the punishment, as I always punished Israel in times past, was so that it may bring them to repentance and may bring healing to their land; that when the people are humbled they would pray to me and I would turn in My mercy, I would forgive them their sins and I would then heal their land. I am going to bring punishment to this nation – a time of humbling – but this punishment is not to destroy this nation. This punishment is to humble her and to chastise her, that she may repent of her wicked ways and turn back to Me.

"There will not be many nations in the days ahead that will be permitted to have what this nation will be permitted to have. You will have a grace and a favour upon you which many other nations will not be given because I have plans and purposes for this country. And even though My own people have been faithless harlots towards Me, know this; that your faithlessness will only go to prove My faithfulness. I will be faithful to My Covenant and to My Word, and I will bring about My ways and My means for this country, and I will pour out My Spirit. And I will bring revival but it will not be like any revival that has been before. It will be uncontainable; it will be uncontrollable; and the world will HATE it because it will be so strong and it will be so powerful that they cannot ignore it.

"In times past they've been able to turn a blind eye to the things of My Spirit but in these days everyone will know about it. Everybody will know about it. The same sun that melts the ice also hardens the clay, and men will drop into two distinct camps: those that love Me and those that absolutely hate Me. This is why in many respects these days are dangerous days because it will polarise people, in ways stronger than they are now; but you will know the righteous and you will know the evil.

"But mark My words, I will do something wonderful with this country; I will restore law and order to this country. This country has become lawless and it has no more order to it. And your Houses of Parliament are an example of the state of your nation, of the division of your nation, of the complexities of your nation. The wickedness and the hardness of heart and the blindness and arrogance of your nation are all set to display, for all the world to see in your own Houses of Parliament. But I am going to do a new thing. And many men will lay down their crowns and place down their swords before Me and repent and give their lives to me. And many powerful men and women who vehemently hate My name, will come to know Me and love My name.

"And some Christians might say, 'Why, why Lord did you save them? They're the ones who brought such depravity to our nation. Why did you allow it?' Because that's My grace, that's My mercy. The very ones that brought in those laws, I will turn into trophies of grace to make the enemy despised in his own camp, for I will make those who passed those wicked laws be the ones that undo them, for they will reveal the secrets and the dark intent and heart of sinful wicked flesh. The world, or this country at least, will look on in horror at the things that they've released and allowed in this country, and they will be rescinded and retracted.

"My people, you need to do this: you need to be spending these hours – because it is only hours – you need to be spending these hours in prayer; you need to be spending these hours on your knees; you need to be spending this time in the Word, learning from Me, learning from My Spirit and I will teach you many wonderful things. But this is the time because there are many bridesmaids out there that do not have enough oil in their lamp and you need to get it in your lamp. No-one can part-exchange their life of intimacy with Me to those that have no intimacy with Me. This is your chance; now is the time to do it, for in the humbling that's coming – this wind of change that's going to blow through this land – it's going to be a difficult time for this nation. It will not be a long time, but the depth of the punishment that will come will be severe, even though it will only be for a short time. It was like when I said to King David, "You can have three years of this, three months of that, or three days of the other."

"This will be a short punishment but it will be a deep punishment; a deep chastisement to this nation. And I will humble this nation and I will turn her around. And many who are your enemies in these days will become your friends and neighbours in the days to come.

"So be prepared, be encouraged but be warned; this is not going to be an easy day that is coming, it is going to be a difficult day, a difficult time for this nation. Many Christians will cry out, 'Why did you allow such things to come to this nation?' But in part, everyone in this nation is responsible for the punishments that are coming.

"There is much worldliness in My Body, much worldliness in My Church, much worldliness in the mindset of Christians, much worldliness in the teachings of the Church! They have apostatised; they have become an apostate church, in that they've drifted away from the truth of scripture and have chosen to allow the doctrines of men to infiltrate the teachings of the Church. The sacred scriptures should never be changed, never diluted, never touched, never altered, for they are sacred and they are from the throne room of heaven itself. How dare man place his DNA and his ideas over that which is heavenly and beyond?

"So take heart to these words and this warning. Be blessed, be encouraged and get ready, for the time is now when the humbling must begin. And it will be short but long. It will be a short period of time but it will feel like the longest period of time, for it will be very intense. And for a period of three years a time of great humbling will come upon this nation, and it will be a heavy three years, a very difficult three years.

"But then things will change, things will turn, and you will go from Winter to Spring, Spring to Summer, Summer into Harvest time."

Christopher Wickland 28th of November 2019

The three blessings and the three woes

My name is Christopher Wickland, I've been a Christian going on for nearly 30 years. Over that time I have received many visions and dreams I believe to be from the Lord. Some of those visions and dreams have impacted and literally saved peoples lives.

There has been many words and dreams I have held onto for a long time, over 20 years regarding the war with Iran, the great economic collapse and the Great Revival. All of these words in the time I received them were very much out of time in respect to the world's then geopolitical climate.

I feel now is the time to start opening up these words and revealing them to the general public for those who wish to hear such things. This word I am about to give will contain elements of those words including new prophetic insights I believe the Lord has given to me.

This prophetic word will be broken into two sections. A message of woe and a message of hope.

I need to make it clear, that I do not live to be a sensationalist, to grab attention or to be one who seeks stardom in the small world of the prophetic. On the contrary, I wish to be one who would rather hide in the shadows and remain hidden. I would rather live out my life in peace with God and man. It brings me no joy whatsoever to bring prophetic words, especially weighty ones.

<u>MESSAGE OF WOE</u>

The First Woe

The first part of this prophecy is aimed at the Stone Wall in our government. This is for those who have ears to hear, and have understanding to what the Spirit is saying.

"Oh Stone Wall. You have become great and marvellous in the eyes of man. You have grown from a child to a man. You have become as a king, dictating your edicts across this land with pride and arrogance. But know this. I never put you where you are today. I have allowed you to become the size you are so that I may bring you down with a mighty fall. I will chop down the tree of your influence. I will not even permit a stump to remain. I will utterly wipe the memory of you from this land.

"I am the Lord of breakthrough and I will shatter you Stone Wall. You think you are impenetrable, you think no one sees or knows. But I see, I know and to me you are as a grain of sand. I will destroy you Stone Wall and I will grind you to dust. You will never rise again and never again put your edicts and rules over this land again."

The Second Woe

"I have declared a wind of change to blow through this nation. This wind is cold, sharp and bitter and it will tear down the institutions and arrogance of man. To My people I say, do not fear this wind. This must come before revival. I will clear the rubble of the empires of man before I will rise the Kingdom of My Name.

"My people, do not fear. I have not failed or forsaken you. I am with you always to the end of the Age. My wind of change will blow through government and establishments that no longer revere or respect My Name. I will shake all that can be shaken so that what remains will be made strong and intact.

"This wind will bring great shaking to the financial institutions of this land, indeed it will spread out to the whole world. For a season the systems of Babylon must be restrained. My people it is time for you to come out of Babylon and its time for Babylon to come out of My people.

"The wind of change will be painful but not unbearable. Great shaking and change is about to come upon this nation. My people do not fear this wind, for this is of My doing.

"I will shake all that can be shaken, even the institutions within my church. Many will fall in this hour from lofty hights and many in the mud will be raised up. Do not be surprised by this. Many will be surprised by what gets pulled down and what remains. Some may become shocked at what I choose to raise up in the days ahead."

The Third Woe

"War is coming and it's time to be prepared and not be troubled by this. I need to warn my people that this is not the battle of Gog and Magog. Many will claim it is, but it is not. Take comfort in this.

"A perfect storm is coming. <u>War with Iran will be inevitable</u>. America will be the first <u>to fire back</u>. This will escalate into a protracted season of conflict that will affect the nations.

"This war will cause the rise of militant Islam to take a hold in this country. Great fear will grab this nation as they realise they have an enemy within that they cannot see. But I want my people in this hour to not fear. Yes, some persecution will come from Islam to my people in this country. But it will be for a short season and then it will end."

MESSAGE OF HOPE AND BLESSING

The First Blessing

"Many will question why I let the three woes come about. Many will point the finger at Me and wonder why. Let me be clear, the finger of blame lies within your governments. They have polluted this land with doctrines and laws that are not of me. The prayers of the saints have come up to me and I have heard those prayers.

"The three woes are not to harm my people, they are part of the dismantling of the profane, that good may rise from the ashes.

"The First blessing is growth. I will bring a new season of Spring to this nation. Once the bitter wind of change has blown its course, new life will come to this nation again. I love your green and pleasant land and I wish to use you as a sheep nation in these days. I chose to use you as a mighty oak in the orchard of the nations to be blessed to be a blessing to those around you.

"You will be instrumental in standing shoulder to shoulder with Israel. I will bless you, to enable you to stand with her and I will bless you greatly for standing with her."

The Second Blessing

"The Second blessing will be a religious revival in the land of Great Britain. Churches will come to life and grow throughout all the land. It will be as in the days of Wesley. Churches will spring up in every city, village and town.

"I will do outlandish and interesting things. I will raise up again monastic houses of prayer and prayer communities throughout this nation to pray for the land of Britain. To work the land and bless the land that healing may come to the soil. I will heal the land for all the pollution of sin and wickedness that has corrupted it.

"In these days I will move in great power, signs and wonders will be seen by many. These will be days of open heavens and many will come to know me as they sense my presence filling up this land. My presence will be as a wonderful incense. It will permeate this land and all will sense it. All will breath it in and be changed by it. In these days many, many will give their lives to me.

"This is a blessing with a great charge. My people be ready for this harvest. Don't ever turn people away. Move with me, don't move against me because of fear. Be prepared to move into uncharted waters in these days in respect to church growth."

The Third Blessing

"I will make this nation a head and not a tail. I will raise her up in the days ahead because I have plans for this nation. Plans to prosper and not plans to harm.

"I have remembered the prayers of this nation that have come before me for over a thousand years. They will not go unheeded or unanswered. I will beautify My Name in this Land again.

"Many will read this and wonder how such things can be. Wait and see for the Lord is good and His promises shall not tarry but surely come to pass.

"This nation will have in this blessing a strong, trusted and godly government that walks on the foundations of my Word. The government of this land will once again be respected and appreciated. It will no longer be a laughing stock. Indeed I will make it so that the former days will not be brought to remembrance.

"Do not fear my flock, do not be afraid. Be prepared for a winter of discontent. Set your faces like flint for the Spring that is soon to follow.

I promise you that I will protect you and provide for you. Do not be afraid, only believe. You are going to see the goodness of My Name in the land of the living."

Published 18th September 2019.

The English Oak

"I want My people who are called by My Name to hear My voice in this season.

"Do not be perturbed, disturbed or ruffled by what you see and hear in your nation at this time. I am the Lord your God, I love you and I am with you. I will not fail or forsake you.

"Hold on tight to my promises as the road ahead will get bumpy. Things are going to take a serious turn over the next few months. There will come some violent shakings that are so severe even those most asleep will be jolted out of their slumber.

"Remember the story of Peter walking on water. If you look to the left and the right you will surely start to sink. But I promise if you keep your eyes upon Me and My promises, I will surely hold you aloft. My mercy and grace is sufficient for you. Even if you do start to sink, merely call upon Me and I will assist you.

"Beware the doomsayers, who proclaim their chastisements upon this nation with no hope of deliverance. Yes I do bring shakings and I do bring calamity, but this is for your hope and your future, not your destruction.

"I have plans for this nation of Britain. I will unite and make her great again. Not because of the wisdom of man. Rather it will be through My Spirit as it sweeps away the old and ushers in the new.

"I wish to plant and build, but first I need to tear down and destroy the old. New wine needs new wineskins. A new move of My Spirit needs fresh houses and institutions to work through. The old has become tired and weak. It is sadly of no use to me.

"The English Oak of Britain will be pruned, but not to harm her. Rather the old branches and deadwood needs to be removed and burnt up. I want this old oak pruned so that it will sprout new life and flourish once again. Britain the mighty oak of old will have new life and fervour once again.

"I will restore the ancient paths of this land, the old ways of faith and valour will grow strong after the tearing down and pruning. I will establish My laws and My ways again and make your land green and pleasant once again.

"Oh Britain you mighty old english oak. I must prune you now. But do not be afraid and do not fear. Hold on tight to Me and I will never forsake you or let you go. Although pruning is painful, you need to know my heart is for you to be blessed. My heart and will is for you to once again become a mighty oak as of old. I want this weakened nation to become great again.

"The anger and fires of leaders in this land will soon be extinguished. This nation that wishes to pull itself apart will not be permitted to do so. It was Me who united this nation and I will not let that which I brought together be cast asunder by the arrogance of man.

"Church, do not look to the left or to the right in this hour. Keep your eyes fixed on Me. As everything begins to shake, hold My gaze, do not fear, do not be afraid. Even when the ground beneath you shakes, do not take your eyes off Me. I will sustain you and uphold you."

Christopher Wickland 26th of August 2019

The Seasons are Shifting

This prophetic word was given as a sermon by Christopher Wickland on 31st of July 2022

We are going to start with this scripture from Joshua Chapter 1:1-3.

'After the death of Moses, the servant of the Lord, the Lord spoke to Joshua, the son of Nun, Moses' assistant saying 'Moses my servant is dead, now proceed to cross the Jordan you and all these people into the land that I am giving to them the Israelites, every place that the sole of your foot treads upon I have given you as to Moses.'

Now we read those words just very matter of fact; He woke up one day. Moses is dead. Joshua gets a word from God. Moses is dead. I want you now to take on Moses' mantle and we just read that casually and cavalier - blah, blah, whatever. But I just want you to think about that for a second. Moses was probably, up until Jesus, the greatest prophet that ever lived. There was no-one who had done those kinds of signs and wonders. Never in the past. Not Abraham. Nobody. Even by todays standards he ranks pretty high up there. Right? And then the day comes that he has died and with that comes the end of an era. The end of a generation. The end of something everyone had grown up comfortable with.

Moses was this great kind of pastor over the people. But Joshua was a different kind of leader. He was a solider. He was the one normally fighting the battles. When Moses was on the hill holding his arms up and he had his brother and another guy holding his arms up. It was Joshua down on the ground fighting. So Joshua was a man of war and it was Joshua who was raised up by God and called to send the people over the Jordan and into all the land that he was giving to them. Joshua's job was to get the Old Testament 'church' out of the wilderness and finally into the land of Israel or the land of promise.

This week God has been showing me a vision of a big clock. A giant clock. And you've got those cogs and things turning around. And we've been in various different seasons of the church over the last 100 years or so. But what I felt God saying was that the clock is about to change and we are now just on the threshold of the next hour. And when this big cog turns then the link pin thing clicks in place and then the hour hand clicks in place and we are now about to come into a new hour, a new season.

Moses my servant is dead. The old ways of doing stuff is soon about to become utterly obsolete in ways that are shocking in the things of the world. You are going to see in parallel here what goes on in the church and what's going on in the world and what's going on in the world with what goes on in the church because judgement starts with the House of the Lord. Does it not say that? So there are things that are coming to the house of the Lord that are going to be mirrored with things that are going on in the world. And some of the things that are going to happen in the world like for the Israelites to wake up and find that Moses is dead and this whole new… well that's all we've ever known and where are we going now? And Joshua? He's alright. He's a good guy. Where are we going with him? He's not done all these signs and wonders. And so people are going to wake up very soon to a world where the old system is over. And the clock is just about to tick.

And I felt the Spirit say…. (Again this is predictive and I've been used by God to do predictive prophecy before. God used me in 2007 to predict the exact day of the stock market crash 3 months before it happened.). And in this I felt the Spirit was saying that literally on midnight of the first day of autumn of this year the clock will change into the next hour. It's not going by an Israeli system or an Israeli clock or calendar but by the British clock and the British calendar because God has a plan for Britain that is specific for Britain.

And on that moment and on that hour when we suddenly hit autumn at midnight of that night, the new season has shifted and we now walk in the beginning of that new season. When you come out of one season into another one, the effects aren't immediately obvious are they? So when you go from Spring into Summer, you don't just wake up one day and say 'Wow, thank goodness all that rain is over now and it's Summer. Here we go. Get all the kit off and go down the beach.' It's not like that. There's a phase. But something has changed and nature reflects that. So what we are going to see now is trees that are slowly going to start losing their leaves. What you are going to see in the things of the world, you're going to see the systems of this world starting to fail. And you're going to see some incredulous things in these days.

There is going to come things that really shock the church. The Spirit said to me a little while back that there's something coming that is going to make the church reel and stagger with shock and what's coming is that you are going to see a lot of the church in the next two years, a lot of the established churches or great denominations are going to vanish. Just simply going to vanish. Why is this? Because as Moses said to Pharaoh 'Let my people go.' But the problem is, as the people, the Israelites, they left Egypt, the problem is, even after the complete destruction of Egypt. Because it says that God made a public spectacle of the Egyptian gods. He devastated the economy of that land, he devastated the military of that land. He devastated the religion of that land. God devastated it. And the Israelites are in the wilderness who still have Egypt in their heart. And they are like 'If only we could get back to where we were.' Do you want to know why they were crying and groping and groaning about that? Because life was tough. When you go into the wilderness. Life is tough. And life for the church is going to get tough because of the things we are coming into.

This new season is a wonderful season but with it will come change and much consternation and you are going to see some things that are going to happen to this nation economically that are just going to leave most Christians reeling and staggering in shock. But this is a message of hope. This isn't a message of doom and gloom. God is going to do some great stuff and I'm going to get to that in a minute but God wants to make it very clear to people that things are going to drastically change. From autumn this year, the season has changed. Everything will change. This is a complete new paradigm both for the church and for the world.

And I just want to say now because the leaves of the trees will start to wither and fall off - I declare to stonewall in the name of Jesus - you are coming down. There are already fissures in your brickwork, already cracks taking place and I declare to you right now and I prophesy in the name of Jesus that you stonewall are coming down and you will be ground to powder and you will never ever rise again. In fact the name or even the mention of your name will be forgotten and you will never rise again and God says you have placed yourself in positions of power in government where I never sent you and you were never elected. You are a coup d'etat and you are coming down. Your days are numbered and as the season changes as it will do from midnight when we come into autumn of this year stonewall and the beginning of the demise of that wall will begin and she will be gone forever.

With it will come the end of liberalism, hyper liberalism. Hyper liberalism will come to a close because it is the malaise of an affluent society looking for a righteous cause that it can't find because it's too fat and affluent and it's become deceived in its own way and it's gone, not God's way, but her own ways. The agenda of the highly liberal left will collapse and fall in these days . The economical systems of our land are going to fall in these days. The government of our land is going to fall in these days.

But as God tears away the veil of lasciviousness from this nation, this nation will start to turn back to her God again. This nation will start looking to Jesus again. And it will be in these days and this hour that the church needs to be ready. But the problem is with the church that she has too much Egypt inside of her. Every one in this room, we have Egypt inside of us. It's in our hearts. I don't care how radical you think you are for Christ.

You have Egypt in your heart. And it's like a tapeworm and God is going to have to take that tapeworm out. Some of its going to be big and gross and some of its going to be little slithers here and there. But we all have Egypt in our hearts and God is going to remove it from our hearts because God is looking for a pure church in these days. And because much of the church (this is not me judging the church, this is just a fact) because much of the church has built her systems on the systems of Egypt, when God pulls the people out of Egypt and those Egyptian systems are pulled free from the church, many churches will collapse in that hour. This is not Gods heart. This is not Gods will and I felt the spirit also say this morning 'Don't ever rejoice over the downfall of your brothers and sisters in those organisations and those churches. It's not something you should rejoice at. It's something we should grieve for because they made mistakes. We all make mistakes. There was too much Egypt in their systems. There was too much Egypt in their hearts and once Egypt was pulled, because God is saying 'Let my people go'.

Do you think everybody in Egypt wanted to go? I mean it was a mighty inconvenience. All of those people being told by God, however many there was, they reckon about 1.2, to 2.2 million. It was a lot of people. Being told to get out and start moving into their promised land. God tested the saints when they came out of Egypt. They were brought into the wilderness and He tested them. To see what was in their hearts.

We have had a mini test through covid where God squeezed our hearts a little bit to see what was in there. To see how much the body of Christ would really compromise when the pressure was on. And the curtains were pulled wide and the veil of our hearts were laid bare. It was frightening to see people's hearts exposed like that. The people who came to church maybe half of the year, were not really into church, because it was never really a thing. When covid came the excuse that, I don't have to go anymore because really in their heart of hearts they didn't value the importance of church and the community of believers, so for them it was a good excuse to opt out and never come back. And that was just a little thing.

When God took the Israelites into the wilderness He deliberately tested them. He gave them days where they didn't eat and He gave them days where they couldn't drink. And what did they do? This huge column of smoke by day and a huge pillar of fire by night. The Holy Spirit was with them, they could see His presence, they could feel His glory, they saw the miracles. They saw the signs and the wonders and yet they still grumbled at the leaders and they still grumbled at God and God tested them in that place. This is a time church where we can't afford to get it wrong because there is a shaking that is now coming.

You see all that can be shaken will be shaken. 'But I'm a Christian. I'm of a kingdom that can't be shaken.' Yes! But how much of the kingdom is in you verses the kingdom of the world? And the more of the world that is in you, the more you are going to be shaken. And so in this hour God is calling His church and saying 'Now is the time my beautiful church, now is the time to rise. Now is not the time to cower and be afraid but to rise up, to be strong and to be victorious. For the Lord your God is with you. I am behind you, I am above you, I am beneath you and I go ahead of you and I go to lead you into the promised land. The promised land of revival which has been prophesied over this nation for so long.

And the glory of my Spirit will go ahead of you as it did with the Old Testament 'church' but we cannot afford in these days to gripe and groan and complain. This will be a time where people trying to undermine church leaders and things like that will not be tolerated because the move of the Spirit is going to be so strong. And now this is a warning to leaders as well because they don't just get an easy ride here. The Spirit has things to say to church leaders in this moment as well. When God was moving in the Book of Acts there was a beautiful revival going on there and people were selling their property and giving it to the apostles so that it could be distributed to help everyone. And we had Ananias and Sapphire who willingly lied in the midst of a move of God. And the Holy Spirit is really saying that in this new move of the Spirit there will be no tolerance of this kind of behaviour. God is a good God and he loves you but the move that is coming is going to be so precious and so powerful that he can't afford people to undermine His work. There will be no tolerance for leaders that try to control it and manipulate it and call it their own work. This will be a place for humility.

God is calling His church into a new season. This season - God gave me this vision years ago. I know I've shared this many times. It was a waking dream vision. And I saw in front of me this big canvas. Like a big graph and it has these dates, these years but they were fudged out and I couldn't see them clearly and I saw this kind of curve and it got bigger and bigger and it shot right up to the top and it was known when it hit the top as 'The Golden Age of the Church.' That curve was the incremental increase of God's glory on the earth from a certain moment in time. That move is now about to come about. Again Autumn is the key to this new season that we are coming into but it will be a season of great shaking and shifting.

You see there are two winds that are blowing. First comes the wind of holiness, then comes the wind of power. And if you don't turn into the wind of holiness you can have no part in the wind of power. God wants to bring power back to his church again. God wants there to be signs and wonders. And we are going to see it exponentially in the days coming ahead but we must turn into that first wind. And that first wind is not comfortable. No one wants to know how much of a sinner they are. No one wants to talk about it. Churches won't even talk about sin any more because it's just not politically correct. It's more about getting the numbers in. We don't want people going away feeling bad about themselves. We just want big churches because that's what success is today. Sin is a problem to a holy God and God is going to come and start dealing with things in our lives. He is going to start dealing with motivations. And it's going to get mightily uncomfortable.

In Isaiah Chapter 6 - he was stood right in front of the presence of God and what could he say? He falls to his knees and he says, 'Woe is me for I am a man undone. I am a man of unclean lips.' The holiness of God is coming back to His church and it's going to purify His church and His church is going to be beautiful. It's going to be a beautiful, beautiful church. It is not going to be a church like you think it might be. It's not going to be a church you might even expect or hope it to be. It's going to be a very different church. God said to me a long time ago that He is going to blend the Spirit and the word together and He is going to blend the ancient and the modern. Ancient church blended with the modern. Have you any idea what that would look like? A lot of charismatics would say 'I'm not getting involved with that. We don't do that kind of stuff.' But God is going to do something outlandish.

And there will be no more time in the future for you to get upset because 'they're catholic or they're orthodox or they're Church of England and all of that nonsense. In the days we are coming into, that kind of division God is not going to be happy with. God wants his church to be one and he wants you to love your brothers and sisters. Because they think you're wrong just as much as you think they are wrong. I can see you thinking, 'But I'm not wrong am I? I couldn't possibly be'. We've got to get over ourselves. The Spirit is going to do some wonderful things. And we are going to see a tremendous revival that is soon to be outpoured.

And here's a message for church leaders. God would say to you - the growth is going to be beyond anything you've ever experienced or anything you could ever dream to cope with. Because two thirds of the church are going to cease to exist soon, the greater pressure is upon that one third left in the UK to cope with that kind of growth. Don't you dare turn people away. Don't you dare say 'This is enough. I'm not doing any more I'm at capacity.' because the spirit of the Lord would say do not think that otherwise I will find someone who can cope. God is looking for leaders that have some gumption, that have some spirit to them. That have some fire. People that will seek Gods face. People who will pray. People who are not lukewarm or half hearted but people who are on fire for Jesus and will say 'Jesus whatever it is that you want me to do 'Here I am send me."

And 'If Lord Jesus you want to send 10,000 people in through that church door then yes I'll probably have a panic attack but Jesus we will get it done somehow. You will give us the wisdom.' How do you think the apostles felt? They had a nice little cosy prayer meeting - 120 in the upper room. This is a good little church we've got going on here. We've got some good numbers and then suddenly the Holy Spirit breaks out and they go from 120 to 3000 people and then we know a few weeks later it then says 5000 men got saved let alone women and children. 'I don't do mega church'. Well good for you but Jesus did in Jerusalem. It's like that church just exploded. You don't hear of anything. You only hear the rumbles and rumours about how certain widows weren't fed correctly. I think they did a pretty good job. 12 leaders in a church of goodness knows how many thousands and then it spread and it spread and it spread. God wants to get Egypt out of His people. God is saying 'Let my people go.'

The institutions of man are going to come down. Lots of things will just come down in these days. But God wants you to be encouraged.

He doesn't want his people to be in fear. He doesn't want his people to be in consternation. God showed me this dream once. It was this kraken. It was this huge octopus thing and it was so disgusting to look at. It made me feel violently ill looking at it. It had these eight tentacles and it was symbolic of the perfect storm that hit us. It was economic, it was every single thing all coming at one time. And when I looked at this thing I was terrified. The fear inside of me, it was just tangible fear. And the Spirit of God said 'Why are you afraid of that?' 'Well can't you see what it's doing, it's ripping our nation apart, literally killing people.' and God said 'Why are you afraid of it?' We are not supposed to be frightened. It's a commandment in the scripture 'Do not be afraid.' It's not an optional extra. It's a commandment. God wants us to be brave in the days ahead. Yes there will be much consternation. Yes there will be much sadness as we see many large churches disappear over the next couple of years but God is wanting to move through his people.

God is wanting to do a new thing. And the Spirit of God is coming brothers and sisters. It will be unlike anything else you've seen. But it's going to last for a window of time. It will only be for about 20 years. We will hit the golden age of the church where churches will literally meet in football stadiums because football stadiums will be desperate to sell their football stadiums because they won't be able to use it for anything else because there will be no money to play football like they used to. The church will take back those cultural icons and turn it into something that glorifies God instead of glorifies man. You are going to see the landscape of Britain change.

Now over the next couple of years as the church changes on this topography of shifting sand and you see many churches disappear you will see a resurgence of home churches and house churches. Now there will be many churches that will still stand in these days and they will do well but there will be many who will have to become house churches to keep Christianity going forward whilst there is such a dearth of Christendom throughout the UK. But in time the problem will be those house groups are going to keep growing and growing and growing. "We're going to go underground." (Says the people who want to do underground church) Good for you. That can only last for a little while until you start getting noticed and you will come back up above ground and house churches will have to become bigger churches and regular churches with leadership to help it function. Help it to do well.

Something else I felt the Spirit say this morning as well is that, now this might sound rich coming from me a leader, but I was once not a leader and I know how you feel about what I am about to say but God was showing me through the book of Numbers when there was great grumbling against leadership and there was people thinking 'Well actually I think I should do this job.' All those people, the sons of Korah, who came before Moses and said 'We're fed up with you leading this lot, telling us what to do, prophesying this and giving us the law and only you guys can serve as priests. We can serve as priests as well. Why can't we all do it?' So they got before the Lord and Moses came before the Lord and they had this big meeting and God said Ok sons of Korah get your lavers out so that you can offer a priestly offering to the Lord. And then fire came out from the holy place and completely burned them up and then after this there was another rebellion and the ground literally opened up.

Because what God is going to do is so holy in these days, there will be no toleration any more. God is not going to tolerate churches being pulled down by Jezebels. God will not tolerate those people any more. In the book of Revelation it talks about Jezebel doesn't it? Jesus says I'm going to put her on a bed of sickness if she doesn't repent. She will die. We are moving into a time….. you might think this isn't very full of grace. This isn't the Jesus I know. Actually this is the Jesus you know. And when God is moving in power, remarkable things happen. The Holy Spirit will not be mocked in these days we are coming into. It's a precious move of God.

Now what's going to happen to the politics of our land? The land of Great Britain is going to look very different. The politics of a conservative, a labour, a liberal are going to be meaningless very soon. God is going to raise up a different government. People are getting tired of the same old same old and the Spirit of God is tired of the same old same old and the heinous laws that have been passed over this land that have profaned this land with its filth. There have been things that have taken away the innocence of our children in schools and this will all stop. Technology has pushed things too far and this too will stop. It will not be permitted to go where some think it will go. And this government as it stands will not last. Parliament as we know it will collapse on itself and she will not last. But from chaos and from that rubble will come a new parliament. One that's not about popularity contests. One that's not about how awesome I am but one that's based on the rule of law. It will not necessarily be a Christian government but there will be many righteous people in it. The people that run it will be people of principle. They will be putting the needs of the Country first not the needs of their own political career first.

But again this is only for a season, a window and this is the message that God wants to say to his church and his church leaders. You have 20 years. You have 20 years opportunity to build this church bigger than anything you could ever dream or imagine. The Spirit of God is going before His people as a pillar of smoke by day and as a pillar of fire by night and we are going to follow Him out and He is going to lead us into new territory and He is going to lead us into new places. For the Israelites when they came out of Egypt they'd never experienced this form of God before, they had no revelation of this kind of God before. They received the Torah at Mount Sinai. They'd never received anything like that before. They'd never seen anything like that. And it's the same with the church and where she's going. There will be things that you have never seen before. Now God won't change the Word of God - that is unalterable - but there will be things and experiences that you have never seen and you have never experienced that you're going to be coming into.

And God wants His Bride ready. God wants his people equipped because saints - we are at war. There is a war going on right now. We are the church militant and we have a battle to contend with. We have an enemy to take down. We don't wrestle against flesh and blood but against powers and principalities and rulers and dominions in heavenly places and our job is to start taking the kingdom again back out to the world. But not with words and not with apologetics and not with the cleverness and wisdom of man but with the power. Because the gospel is the power of God unto salvation to those that believe. You're going to see evangelists rise up again in this land.

You're going to see tent crusades spreading the whole of the UK like they did back in the 40s and 50s and the 60s. You are going to see a revival and a resurgence of the evangelists again in this land. You are going to see a resurgence of Josephs in this land. People who are appointed by God for this moment, for this hour to help the church through the most difficult time of modern times.

There is a financial famine and a spiritual famine. God is going to raise us those Josephs to help lead the church at this time. God is going to raise up beautiful pastors who will lead his people. God is going to raise up great bible teachers in this day as well and God is going to raise up church fathers in this day. For the generation of church fathers are almost gone. Our previous generation are dying away. We have not many left but God is going to raise up some new people. Some greats. Hallelujah.

I feel the Spirit also says that people say 'In this revival there will be no leaders, there will be no superstars.' You're right there won't be any superstars as you understand it per se but there will be great men and women of God and they will be used by God to lead his people because God is immutable. That's how he has always done it and he isn't going to change because it's a manifestation of kingdom on the earth. It's a manifestation of the kingdom in the heavens. God the Father, through His Son, via the Spirit, down through the angelic host, down on to the earth. There is order. There is principal. There is leadership. There is governance in His church. In heaven and on earth. Hallelujah. You're going to see Catholic, Protestant, Orthodox rubbing shoulders, standing shoulder to shoulder in solidarity, in love for one another, not picking holes in one another. There is coming a unison of the Spirit that will surpass any theology, that will surpass any of our natural knowledge that you would like to argue about. Those things will not matter in the days ahead because He who is with you, is not against you. And your God is for you and He is not against you.

The time clock is now on the cusp and everything is about to change. When you see war break out further in Europe and when you see stock markets start to shake and tremble and fall, do not be dismayed for the Lord would say to you 'Hold up your head high because you now know that unless this happens God's revival cannot come to this land.' Unless this land is shaken to its core and the people humbled then they will never turn to the Living God. And some people will question the Living God and say, 'Why, why would you let this happen? It's a cruel and mean thing.' ' No it's the best thing I could ever do.' I believe the Lord is saying for this nation otherwise they would never turn to Me and they would never be saved and they would never know the truth and the power and glory of my gospel and the beauty of my son and the power of the Spirit of God.

Sadly there are many in the church that don't want to see these days either. But there are those that do and there's a line that just been crossed today and God is looking for an army. But of course it's going to be Gideon's army. It's not going to be a big army. It's going to be a small army. Because God wants to use the despised and shameful things of this world to shame the wise.

There are new leaders that are coming to the fore. You are going to see batons passed from leaders of old to new leaders. You are going to see household leaders of Christendom vanish and new ones emerge but the message that is going to be given in these times is a controversial message. Why? Back in the days when America was being founded a lot of preachers they rode out and part of their messages was to tell the people who were British in America to come out of British rule and let America become a sovereign state in her own right. That was a radical message in its day and there's going to be a radical message given in this day which may seem devisive but actually it's not. It's the sound that needs to be heard for the hour which we are about to come into because it's a relevant prophetic message. Just as those preachers back in the time were giving a relevant prophetic message that America needed to become a sovereign nation under God and not come under British rule. And so there is a message coming out of the church that will come out in these days that will seem radical and offensive to many but it is a message of reconciliation and it's a message that is saying - the old wineskin doesn't work any more. Put it down. Throw it away. The old ways are over. It's time for a new season. A fresh anointing. A fresh move of God's Holy Spirit. To do things in ways we've never done it before. To go places we've never gone before.

God wants His people to be strong in this day. And the spirit of God is saying 'Who is going to be in Gideon's army?' 'Who is going to put their hand up and say, 'Yes. Here I am send me.?' and God would say the best requirements for you is this….. Some may say I can't do it because I'm too old. You're hired. Some might say I can't do it because I'm too young. You're hired. Some might say I've got too many personal issues. Great. Come on board. Some might say, 'I've lived a terrible life, God how could you ever use someone like me?' and the Spirit of God would say, 'We did it through David and he had all of those cantankerous men that came to him and we turned them into mighty men of God. So you're hired. Come.'

But people who say, 'Hire me Lord. I really know my theology.' 'Jesus without me you just aren't gonna go nowhere.' 'Jesus you need me because I'm a great musician.' 'Jesus you need me because I'm so awesome. I'm such a great church leader.' No! 'Those that lap the water with their tongue. The weirdos. Come over here' and God is going to raise a generation of ragtag, weirdos strange people that God is going to turn like David's mighty men. People that literally changed history.

This prophetic word was given as a sermon by Christopher Wickland on 31st of July 2022

Signs in the Sun

On Wednesday 27th May 2020 pastor Christopher posted this alarm or warning on what's soon to hit the world.   As with all prophecies, please seek the Lord in weighing this vision.

In NKJV, Christopher's Luke reference is headed *'The Coming of the Son of Man':*

"Welcome to another thought for the day. Today I have quite a serious message and one which probably many Christians will find a little bit hard to stomach. I will start with this piece of scripture, then I will get straight into it.

"It says in Luke 21 from verse 25: *"There will be signs in the sun, in the moon and in the stars and on the earth, distress of nations with perplexity, the sea and the waves roaring. Men's hearts failing them from fear and expectation of things coming upon the earth because the powers of heaven will be shaken. Then they will see the Son of Man coming in a cloud with power and great glory."*

"The other night I was out for a walk with my wife, and the Holy Spirit really came upon me suddenly. Something happened there and one of these things that happened was that really strongly the Holy Spirit said to me, *"There will be signs in the sun very soon."*

"Then he reminded me of something that happened to me, probably about 12 years ago. I was on the train going to Portsmouth Grammar School, where I taught at the time in those days, and as I was on the train I fell into like a trance. I know it sounds really weird, but it was a state between sleep and being awake. I remember looking up at the sun, and suddenly the sun changed colour from yellow to green, and there was an ear-shattering crack of thunder across the whole sky, and then the people of the city that I was stood in panicked. I was looking around, with people running and screaming because of this cosmic sign in the sky, and people were terrified and in fear. And then BOOM, I suddenly came to with a start.

"I believe the time is coming now, I believe the Holy Spirit was saying to me, even this morning while I was in the shower, *"Tell the people that the Sign in the Sun is about to start."* And I don't know whether that will be soon, as in like weeks, months, or even years….I don't know. But I believe the Holy Spirit said to me that the signs in the sun will start to commence.
"This will be something, I believe, on a world-wide level – everybody will see it – *and it will defy the laws of physics!*

"The sun will do stuff that the sun just shouldn't do!!
"And this is a sign, both to the nations and a sign to the Church. And it's a sign to the nations that they have to repent. And it's a sign to the Church that we too need to repent and actually get on our knees, and really take seriously the times in which we are living in, because the times that we're living in are more wicked and more dangerous than we actually can even conceive.
"We are like frogs…We are being put in a little bowl of water, and the water has got hotter and hotter, and we as Christians are being boiled alive right now, but we don't even know it. This is a reality of where are at.
"During this time of lockdown I have really been seeking God's face a lot more. And the thing that I'm becoming more and more impressed with by the Spirit is that we are in trouble; in that our nation has turned to such liberalism, where we justify the murder of innocents, where we justify taking away the virginity of our children in their minds, where we justify so many wicked things, where the laws of the land have become an abomination to the things of God and His Word. Where now even churches are turning in droves away from the things of the Gospel and moving into the things of liberalism and of the world. We are in great trouble!

"Now I know a lot of you watching this are thinking, "Woah! This guy, he's lost the plot." Maybe I have, I don't know. But I have to be faithful to what I believe God is showing me, and I remember so vividly that vision of the sun changing colour, and the crack of thunder that ricocheted across the sky, and the *terror* that fell upon everybody.

"Because God is a good God, why would He do such a cataclysmic sign? Well for the Church it's to "Wake Up!". And for the world it's "You need to repent. Time is running short. You cannot carry on living in wickedness and depravity much longer before the Great Tribulation comes to you!. *You have to repent. <u>Now</u> is the time!*"

"The Bible says: *'Today, if you hear his voice, do not harden your hearts.'* <u>Now</u> *is* the time. And when those signs, as prophesied, as I read in the opening scripture, in the sun will start to appear signs and I believe they are coming soon -- then it is a time of warning for the Church, because the Church -- we've become indifferent to the things. We look around our world and go, "Yeah, that's okay. We know it's going on."

"But we need to be on our knees. We need to be praying more fervently, more harder, more gut-wrenching, heart-felt prayers at this time in history, now more than any other time in history to date, because we are at the epoch of the most horrendous of things, and we look around and we're not even aware of how horrendous it is because we're acclimatised to the wickedness of the world in which we live in. But the Sign in the Sun will be God's mercy to His Church to wake us up. Now, I don't know if this is months, weeks or even years away. But this is what I believe God showed me, this is what I believe the Holy Spirit told me to say and to warn us: time is running out, and it is a time to take our faith seriously. God bless you."

Christopher Wickland 27th of May 2020

Visions pertaining to the end of days

This is a transcript of audio from a presentation Chris Wickland gave on YouTube.

"My name is Pastor Chris Wickland and I want to share with you some visions and dreams the Lord has given me a long time ago that I've never shared publicly with anybody, but I feel now is the time to do so and it's pertaining to things regarding the End of the Age, which is not quite yet, but will be soon and I'll unpack and explain that. So today's date is the 15th of February 2023.

Now as you know, back last year towards the end of July I had a prophecy called the shifting seasons and in that word it said that spiritually we were going to go from the Summer time into Autumn time, and with that would come some shakings etc, and this spiritual Autumn would last for a period of around about 15 to 20 years, and in this period of time we will see the church move into great Revival. But there will be great shaking to the Nations and there'll be great shaking in this nation of three specific things. The economy, the government or the political land of this country and also the church. And you know with the things we have seen lately with the church of England, we are seeing that shaking quite clearly coming about. Last night I was going for a walk with my wife and I just felt impressed by the memory of a lot of these visions that God had shown me, that actually we are fast approaching these things and I need to start sharing them.

(SEALED BOOK)

I'm going to put this as a for now as a once off video which I'm going to put out here. I'm not going to heavily promote this, if you find this and you watch this you can make of it as you will. Some of you it will frighten, some of you, I don't know what it will do, but it is quite a serious word, because we are heading into serious days, and the church needs to understand that things unfortunately are not going back to normal. They're not going to get better, they are going to get worse and worse. But in the time of great tumult, will come the greatest of all revivals. Now again some people will take umbrage with that, but please let me explain some of these visions and we'll sort of work our way through it.

One of the dreams that I had was from 20 years ago. I was in this dream and an angel came to me, and he gave me this book, and it had the Seal of the Alpha and the Omega on it. Of course no one could break this seal, I couldn't break it, but the angel could. He had the authority to break it, and he broke the seal, and as he opened the seal, he opened it up, and there I saw what would bring in the age of winter upon the earth.

What's interesting about that is as I prophesied last year about this changing seasons going to Autumn, I realised that God has already revealed to me what the spiritual winter will look like, and what's going to actually be the sign that will usher in the spiritual winter. The sign that was shown in this book, was a large meteorite hitting the earth. It landed in the jungle somewhere and it got national and international press coverage. It didn't cause a lot of damage, but it was certainly newsworthy on an international scale.

Now at our present time, there are lots of fireballs flying across the sky. Do a YouTube search for Fireballs in the sky. They are being reported all around the world. Yet the specific sign the angel told me in this dream, was that when the world would come to a spiritual winter, that would be when one of these fireballs would hit the ground. That would then start a series of them. When that happens, then a spiritual winter would commence and cover the Earth. It would be a time of great spiritual cold. It's not a literal cold, rather a spiritual cold and evil that will be permitted to come to its fullness.

Remember what Jesus taught in his parable of the wheat and the tares. We see both the tares and the wheat come to the fullness of maturity, and so in this time of spiritual winter, evil will come to the fullness of maturity. It will be that future spiritual winter that I personally believe will usher in the rule of the **Antichrist.**

Some of you may think, 'I don't believe any of that nonsense.' However, I'm putting this out on record now, so when these things come to pass and I believe they will, and you see them, hopefully you will remember this and maybe it will wake you up to realise that maybe just possibly there really will be an Antichrist.

One of the dreams that God gave me a long time ago, was when He showed me a graph, and at the bottom of the graph there were dates. These dates were blurred out and then God showed me this incremental curve. At the beginning of the curve it was just a flat-line, and then it slowly started to go up and up until it suddenly shot straight up. When it reached the top, there were words written over it saying, 'The Golden Age of the Church.'

This golden age only lasted for a moment, for a short while and then it suddenly just dropped to zero. When the line flatlines to zero, this will be the spiritual winter beginning. We are currently within the spiritual Autumn now. Very soon we are going to see God start to move more and more. What's been happening in Asbury at the moment in Kentucky, is eventually going to become the norm. There will be these pockets of fire everywhere, where Revival is going to break out. Eventually it will become a wildfire that will just consume the world, and that's going to become the norm. So what we're seeing in Asbury and various other places that we're hearing about, this is the beginning of that incremental curve, starting to go up as we head fast towards the Golden Age of the Church.

I must say these things are going to happen quickly and you must not be taken unawares by this. We are moving into a time now where things are accelerating faster and faster than ever before. You're going to see God move quicker than ever before and you're going to see evil increase quicker than you've ever seen before.

It says in the Book of Joel, 'I will pour out my spirit upon All Flesh before the great and terrible day of the Lord.' Spiritually and scripturally I believe that towards the end of the age, we will see a Revival like the world has never seen before as we fast approach the end of days.

One of the dreams that I had many years ago, which I have hardly shared was about the rise of the Antichrist. Some Christians don't believe in any of that end times stuff, so just take it with a pinch of salt, put it on the back burner and maybe come back to it when these things start to come to pass. In this dream, I was in the United Nations building and in the middle there was this round table. There were world leaders and in the middle of this table was one known as the **Man of Peace.** However, he was anything but the Man of Peace. He was actually behind all the wars and atrocities that were going on in the world. This man was causing all manner of troubles but nobody knew it was him, because he was the 'Man of Peace,' yet he was the one that was instigating all the troubles that was going on in the world. The world nations believed he was the key, that he was the leader of eight key Nations. The Anti Christ was the eighth leader of seven. I believe what's written in the Book of Revelation, about the eighth horn ruling the seventh horn. This so called man of peace was instrumental in bringing great trouble upon the Earth, but he was known as the 'Man of Peace.' Nobody knew what he was really like, but in the dream I saw quite clearly that he was a very evil and dangerous man. He was using politics to manipulate the world stage for his agenda. In this room within the United Nations was a huge statue, a bronze statue. This creature had huge claws and massive fangs, it was a huge bronze creature. It was a Beast, and he brought this Beast to life and this Beast was sent out to ravage and destroy the Nations. When I saw this creature terror and dread came over me. I was in absolute terror because I knew the power that this Beast had and it was given to ravage the Nations.

The dream then moved on and showed other scenes. One of the scenes was regarding a political situation where there was a famous Arab leader who had randomly been struck by lightning and it killed him. Sky News reported that he was in state within his house, when suddenly a UFO appeared and it hovered over his house. The UFO hovered over the house for three days and three nights.

All the news stations around the world broadcasted this, but I remember specifically Sky News saying, 'We now know that extraterrestrial life is for real.' I personally believe that this may be the end time delusion that man will be given over to.

I need to say that things like **UFO**s, flying saucers are a key part of my personal testimony. In my testimony on YouTube titled 'From witchcraft to Christ,' I mention about the UFO phenomena and how it is a deceiving lie of the enemy. The Scriptures state that in the end times man will be given over to a mass deception. I think in part this delusion of space loving peace brothers is just a load of nonsense, it's a deception from the devil. This dream could be showing a metaphor or what will really happen, I don't know, but this whole thing about UFOs is something you will need to pay special attention to. Especially with what's going on in the news at the moment with the shooting down of air balloons and other things that they don't know what they're shooting down.

I had this dream of the Anti-Christ twenty five years ago. In that dream I saw technology which didn't exist then. The dream showed me Christians being hunted down by these small machines that had propellers on them and cameras. I now recognise that technology as drone technology today. The Christians in the dream were in hiding and the Anti-christ was hunting them down.

I appreciate some of the stuff that I'm saying here may be frightening, but we must understand this is for the future. God has showed me in my ministry how I will go through three clear distinct phases. The first, which is being a local pastor. The second, where I'm a Joseph who helps the church through the time of financial and spiritual famine that we're currently coming into. The third part of my ministry is for when I am on old man, Here, I go out to this nation and warn the end of days is coming.

Many ask when is all this going to happen? As I have already said, when we have the opening of that seal, the Alpha and the Omega, and one of those fireballs hit the earth in the jungle somewhere. Then that would be the sign when we go from spiritual Autumn into Winter. Yet remember, like the shifting of Seasons we don't just go from Autumn straight to Winter overnight. I think we have got a fifteen to twenty year opportunity where there'll be great shakings and revival.

After this, then comes the spiritual winter, but I need to make it clear that even the spiritual winter may last many years before it leads into the seven years of the tribulation period. So great wisdom needs to be applied here.

I have also had dreams where Iran and I believe China and possibly Russia (not so sure about Russia I didn't really see it in the dreams but I'm assuming it's her) where China and Iran somehow trigger a World War. I saw a dream where America did something wrong. I don't know what it was but it caused a big uproar amongst the Arabs. This then triggered the war where Iran got heavily involved and then that spilled out into a big war.

I have also had dreams about a war in Europe which I believe is now currently (current year of 2023) ongoing. The Russia and Ukraine war I don't think is going to go away, I just think it's going to escalate and get worse. I have seen dreams where China and America start hitting it off in a bad way with each other which escalates. I saw China do something that she didn't want to do, but she had to do it because she had no choice. Nevertheless, it was an act of War as China dumped the American dollar. Currently China purchases up a lot of American debt as well as investing into the dollar. In this particular vision China dropped the dollar and it wiped out America economically. America is strong militarily but this act of China just wiped her out and made her impotent and powerless.

I believe we're going to see a massive shift of superpowers coming and I see what's going on in Europe starting to spill out, and it's going to escalate and cause problems with America and China. Do remember that these visions take a while to unpack and unfold but this is where we're heading for.

Christians may get frightened by all of this but brothers and sisters Jesus said, 'you know there'll be wars and rumours of wars and earthquakes and all these things but these are merely the beginning of birth pangs.' We are commanded not to be afraid because our life here is just transitory. We are here to serve God and to serve his purposes and his kingdom and so we need to get our hearts right before God.

So I believe that we're going to see more conflict with China and America is going to do something bad that will trigger an uproar with the Muslims and Iran's going to get involved in this somehow. Many years ago, God showed me that when this happens a great fear will come, especially over this nation. I do not know if this is for now or if this is for the time of the spiritual winter. A great fear came over the nation because we had a hidden Army that didn't dress in uniform because they were everyday Muslims. Some of them were so angry and incensed by what had happened that they were causing all kinds of trouble in this nation. People were in terror of them and during this season the church will suffer mild persecution from them. I didn't see a massive persecution, but I did see persecution from some of the militant Muslims in our country. Of course not all Muslims were doing this, but there were some who were attacking people, so it put the country into a place of great fear and great terror.

Another dream that God showed me was again pertaining to the very end of days.

I was on a train when this happened, and I fell into what is like a trance-like state. In the vision I was walking down a city street and I looked up to the sun in the sky. The sun had gone a peculiar colour.

It had gone a green and blue colour. Suddenly there was this almighty explosion that came from the sun that ripped through the heavens. The sun didn't explode, but this huge roar of noise came from it and it ricocheted throughout the city causing the ground to heave and pulsate. At the sound of this shockwave people were running, screaming and pandemonium was all around. Then I immediately woke up out of the trance. God had showed me some of the signs that are coming onto the Earth. In Matthew chapter 24, it talks about the signs of the Earth, about how the seas and everything will be going crazy and how man will faint with fear at the things that are coming upon the Earth.

There will be signs on the earth politically, that will bring great shaking, there will be signs on the earth of war and there will be signs in the heavens. There would be signs in the natural and in the spiritual.

I want to encourage you, that in the meantime, before we come into the spiritual winter that although great shakings are coming, so also is the hope of a huge revival. This revival will start small and then expand until eventually the world is on wildfire for Jesus. In that hour many people will get saved and the church will explode in growth, beyond anything we can currently understand or imagine. This revival is going to be tough for so many people because of the sheer size of the growth.

I want to encourage you that when revival comes it will be the worst of times and the best of times. Terrible things are coming and you're going to see a great shaking coming over the next several years in this nation of Great Britain. It's going to get hot with shakings in our government, shakings in our economy and shakings within the church. Yet, whilst all that's going on, fires and pockets of revival will begin to spread and grow throughout the land.

The church will be divided, between woke and awake, it will be split between darkness and light. There will be no more grey. You won't be able to hide in the grey any longer. In those days I recommend you move to the light and be in the light, as Christ is in the light. Amen, so there you go, please prayerfully consider these words. Maybe put them on the back shelf, and as these things come about maybe re-watch this video from time to time. I do genuinely believe these visions are from God, these are not things I have made up. These are visions I have sat on for a very long time and I believe they are important. They are important to share now because of the days in which we're in and because of the signs and the wonders that are coming upon the Earth. These are very interesting days, indeed these are probably the most interesting days Earth will ever see before the rise of the Anti-Christ.

God bless you."

Christopher Wickland 15th of. February 2023

Brexit and warnings and blessings for Great Britain

This is a transcript from a prophecy given on the 25th of November, 2018.

Right, I am about to record what I am saying. I feel that the Lord is wanting me to prophesy something. You see, really I am a prophet in a pastor's clothing, so that really is my primary function, and most of you will never really get to see that much, but there we go.

EU Council and Theresa May's Brexit Deal

Something has happened today which is very significant for us as Britons. The European treaty thing has gone through that they have agreed for their side of things on the Brexit deal and I don't think God is very happy. This is what I must declare. I am just going to say it out loud. You see, when prophets of old would speak, they would not even necessarily go to the nations they spoke to, but they spoke to them because they were releasing the word of the Lord, and word of the Lord will do what He will do. Unfortunately, I have to say this over our government and over our country:

"MENE, MENE, TEKEL, UPHARSIN. God has numbered your kingdom and finished it. You are weighed in the balances and found wanting. Your kingdom is divided and has been given to another." [Daniel 5:25-28]

I just feel God is really not pleased with what has happened this week and what is about to happen. I have had, over the years, many dreams, many visions for about twenty-odd years about what is about to come to this land. And unfortunately, what has happened now has just triggered it, because God led this country to come out of something that He was not happy we were even in to start with. People voted for that. Not only did people vote for that, but He moved people by His Spirit to come out. And yet people who think they are better and know more than the plans and purposes of God have tried to intervene and tried to stop what God has decreed must happen. And because man has put his hatchet on the line, and because man has tried to sabotage the engine of what God was trying to do, God has unfortunately had to bring down the axe of his judgement, and unfortunately it is going to bring a separation from us from Europe, whether we like it or not. But unfortunately, it is going to be costly and it is going to bring our nation to a place of humility.

Humbling Nation and Church

You see, God cannot heal our land until our land has been humbled. "Unless my people humble themselves and pray… then I will not heal their land" [2Chronicles 7:14]. And this land must now come through a time of humbling. This land must come to a place where it will call out to the Lord its God.

"It is a nation that is proud. It is a nation that has become arrogant. It is a nation that has thrown aside my laws and my precepts and thrown aside my Word and thrown aside my people, and thrown aside my church. My church has forsaken my ways. My church has forsaken my laws and my precepts and my holy Word. They have moved to the left when they should have always been in my Kingdom. They should have been teaching the Kingdom, but instead they taught the precepts and the doctrines and the philosophies of man."

"And because of this, I must humble my church as well. There are those that are following me, and they are following me with all their heart. I don't speak to them. I speak to the church that takes my Word and brings mixture to it, and brings worldliness to it, and brings worldly philosophies and worldly ideologies to my Word. No more!"

Humbling Government Institutions

"This country is going to humbled, and unfortunately the institutions which hold this country up are now going to have to topple. The things that this country feels that it has as sure foundations I am now going to take away", says the Lord. "And I will tear away the veil of lasciviousness so this country will finally wake up and look up and see that I alone am God, and I will save all who call upon the name of the Lord."

But if I feel God is saying, "Enough is enough. They have had their time. 'MENE, MENE, TEKEL, UPHARSIN.' You have had your time. You have had your chance. You have had your warnings. But you refused to listen, and you refused to relent, and you refused to repent. And now, I do not want to do what I now have to do, but you chose this. You chose to not follow me. You chose to not follow the voice of the people. You chose not to follow the leading of my people. You chose not to follow the leading of my prophets."

"And I am speaking now to the Government. They have heard the voice of the prophets. They have heard the prayers of the saints that have gone up for this land. They know the petitions of my people, and they have ignored them. And I tell you now, you will not ignore the voice of my prophets in this land anymore. You will now come to a time of humility, and you will be humbled," says the Lord.

"But I have plans for this nation. Yes, she must be humbled, but I will bandage up her wounds. I will take care of her, and I will raise her up, and I will look after her, and all of those that call upon the name of the Lord shall be saved. And I will bring this country into the plans and purposes that I have for it. And I have plans to prosper this country; I do not have plans to harm her."

"But know this: 'MENE, MENE, TEKEL, UPHARSIN.' You have chosen to do it your way, and this night, the kingdom will be taken from you."

Call to Watch and Pray

"But know this, my people, that my plans, my purposes, and the heart of the church praying for revival is now coming about. But you need to hang on, and you need to hang on tight, because everything is going to be shaken, and all which can be shaken will be shaken. And I will shake the hearts of man. I will shake the institutions of man. I will shake the churches of man. I will shake everything, so that all that is left is pure and is holy and is righteous and gives glory to my name."

"And this land will be called great again, not because of the greatness of man, but because of the greatness of my Spirit that sweeps this nation as this nation in humility says, 'Sorry, Lord, we're sorry; we repent, Lord.' When this country, like it did once before in the

Second World War, when they came to days of prayer and they humbled themselves and said, 'God, we cannot do this, we need You to intervene!', I intervened," says the Lord. "Those days will come again. Those churches will be filled. And again, my people will cry out, and the people of this land will cry out, and they will say, 'Save us from what is happening!' And I will hear their prayers, and I will bring my salvation," says the Lord. "Not just salvation of spirit, but salvation of your physical bodies. I will save you from what is coming."

"And the church at large, she is happy-go-lucky. She sees the news, she sees the signs of the times, and she is blind to that which is right in front of her. She is blind, and when this tidal wave comes, and it has now began, when this tidal wave hits this coast, she will go, 'Well we never knew, we never saw this coming; God, why did you let this happen?' And I say to you, church, I told you, I warned you. You saw it in the papers, you saw it on the news. You could not have been blind to it. You knew it was coming. Even if you didn't listen to my prophets, you knew that it was coming. But you chose to ignore it, you chose to brush it under the carpet."

God's Motivation

"And sadly, first, judgement must come to the house of the Lord [1Peter 4:17]. But I only judge that I may raise you up, that I may bless you, that I may help you to walk in the things that I have for you. I am going to do great things in this land. But I am sorry for what you are about to see come upon this nation. I am sorry for what is about to happen to your government. I am sorry about what is about to happen to the institutionalised church. I am sorry about what is going to happen to your economic systems."

"But I do this so that I may bring revival. I do this that I may bring life to this dying country. I do it that I may bring sanity to the insanity of this nation. I do it that I may bring light to the darkness. I do it that I may bring fruitfulness where there is barrenness. Do not look with the eyes of man, and the eyes of mammon. But look with the eyes of the Spirit, and see what I am about to do is a glorious thing and a great thing, for it will glorify me," says the Lord. "But it will humble man."

Hallelujah.

No More Frivolity

So, in the light of, that, one of the things that we need to do… You see, I have been teaching on purpose for a while now about equipping the church about her walking in a place of faith, about walking in a place of intimacy in the things of God, about meditating on Scripture, about getting deeper and deeper into the things of God. Because, if I had said two years ago what I know what is coming, most people would run for the hills, most people would be frightened, most people would be terrified. God doesn't want His people in tumult and in terror. He wants His people to be in a place of being stood on the foundation and rock solid.

And I am telling you now, everything is going to shake. Yes, there will be some that will stumble, but you will get back up again. But what is coming is going to shake us. And this is why we cannot play around with this [tapping his Bible] any more. We can't do this anymore. We can't play around with the silliness of man any more. We can't do it.

And I tell you the truth, the day has now arrived where all of our nonsense is over. Because you will look around and go, 'But, but, but this,' and 'But that'. It will mean nothing tomorrow. It will mean nothing. Because the only thing that matters is this [pointing to the pages of the Bible]. The only thing that matters is the kingdom of God. The only thing that matters is that we are of a kingdom that cannot be shaken [Hebrews 12:28]. That is the only thing that matters. It is the only thing.

'What about my new hairdo? Or what about my new car that I wanted to buy? What about that mortgage I wanted to take out? What about this, and what about that?' Leave it! Leave it! Focus on the things of the kingdom. Focus on the things of God. Because unfortunately the time has now come. And our days of frivolity, our days of just coasting in Christianity, our days of taking it easy and sunbathing in the glory of God is over. It is over.

Holiness of the King

We are now coming into a new season, and it is a season of power. But you see, when God pours out His power, there comes with it a season of responsibility. I remember a pastor friend of mine. He was around... he is still alive now, and he is in his 80s. And he was, when he was a very young lad – so probably about fifteen, sixteen – his pastor had been in the Welsh Revival with Evan Roberts. And so, he would ask him questions about the Welsh Revival. And he said, "So, you know, what did you do all day? I mean, how was it you were just stuck on the floor for hours? What were you doing in there?" Because back in those days they didn't have smoke machines and lights and real awesome things going on, you know. They just had a hymn, a thing, and that was it. He said, "What did you do?" He said, "Well, well really, when the holiness of God turned up," he said, "you went to the floor, and you stayed there. And you didn't move. You wouldn't dare move."

And you know, some of us are going, 'Do I really want to see that in the church? Do I really want to see that?' I remember years ago, I said to God, "O Lord, send revival! Send revival!" And the Holy Spirit said to me so clearly, He said, "There will come a day when you will wish you had never prayed it." Because when you see the holiness of God, when you are in the presence of God in the flesh, the flesh in its current state cannot cope with the power and the presence of Almighty God. When Isaiah was in the presence of God, he was like [bowing his head], "Woe is me, for I am undone! I am a man of unclean lips!" And when the presence of God comes back to the church, it will be unendurable. But it will be glorious! Oh, it will be glorious. And when you see the power of God moving...

And it is not dependent on a man's name on a billboard. It is not down to the great evangelist. It is not down to Great So-and-So and Brother This and Sister That. It is a time for our egos to be burned up. It is a time to put that nonsense aside. It is a time to put away all the 'I want to be a great minister in the things of the kingdom of God, I want to have my name etched in the annals of history'. Forget it! Because we are not here for us. But we are here to serve the purposes of the King. That is all we are here for. We are here to serve our glorious, mighty, mighty King.

Dream of Fire on the Coastlands

I remember one of the first dreams that God ever gave me was:

I was walking down the south coast, and I saw this big hurricane-type thing, tornado thing, coming in from the sea and onto the land. And on the land were all these beach huts just arched around the south coast. And this column of wind turned into a column of fire, and it just [clapping his hands together] smashed into all these beach huts. And these beach huts were all the ministries and all the churches and all the institutions that were built in the name of Jesus but were actually built in the name and for the glory of man. And [clapping his hands together] one by one by one, they were disintegrated and vaporised by the heat of God's power and God's glory. And I ran for my life, and I could feel the searing heat of this fire burning across my face as I had to get away from it, as it was consuming everything that was not of God. All those ministries that claim to be of God, all of those churches that claim to be of God, He just burned them all up – [clapping his hands together] bang, bang, bang, bang, bang. And then eventually, there was this house made of stone, down the end of the shore, and the cloud of God's glory came down and descended upon it. And the house was disappeared in all of this fire. But then the fire lifted, and I was taken inside this house. And as I was inside the house – it looked like a building like this sort of size [gesturing to his own surroundings] – and all the walls were encrusted in gems and gold and silver, because God had purified His church. And it was the glory of God that purified His church. You see, every single piece of diamond, every crustation of semi-precious stones and precious stones in the wall, is His people, that were all purified and set on display by the power and the glory and the majesty of God.

Grace, Holiness and Unity

And God is coming back to town, and He wants His church back. And He is taking the hands of man off that which belongs to Him. He is taking the hands of man off that which is sacred, and that which is holy. God is bringing holiness back to the church again. The days of running into church like the Flappers from the '40s, where we are just like, 'Haha, I am just going to be exuberant, and like this, and I am just going to say it, and I am transgender! And all these things!' When they come into the presence of Almighty God they will fall to their knees, and cry out, 'Woe is me, I am before a holy God!' And God will change them, God will save them, God will set them free. And the lies and the philosophies of man will be dealt with, with a punishing blow.

We serve a wonderful God. Jesus loves us. The message of grace we have had for the last twenty years is a powerful, beautiful message. But everything comes in seasons. And the season that we have to move into now, because of the severity of what we are coming into, is... We will always be under God's grace, but we are moving into a new season, a season of holiness. It is not just about the holiness of God. It is about our holiness. It is about us being separated to God. It is about us learning to love one another, and accept one another, and not judge one another. That we do all things in the light of His glory, and in the light of the revelation of Christ, and not our ideas. You see, when you behold the glory of God, when you behold the vision of Christ, when you behold God in such a way that you know Him like that, when you look at yourself and you look at others, everything that you are pales into insignificance compared to Him. And therefore, you are in no place to judge another believer. You are all in this together.

And you see, this is the irony, this will be what will unite His church. This is all prophetic. You see, this church is a Methodist church. But it won't be soon. There are Church of Englands out there, there are Pentecostal churches, there are charismatic churches out there, there are Baptist churches out there, but there won't be soon. There will just be 'the Church'. Because all of those things will be torn down. The Methodist symbol will be ripped down. The Church of England will be ripped down. The Pentecostals, we'll rip it all down, because we are all in this together, because we all worship and serve the same God. And as a sign of the times, of the end of days, the prayer of John 17 will finally come to pass, when Jesus said, "I pray that my people will be one, even as We are one".

And we will see a new Church rise up. We will see, from the destruction of all that we hold dear around us, from the destruction of what even we thought was Christian, as it all falls to the ground and lies doomed in ashes, then we see that building where the glory of God came on it, and then raised it. We see this wonderful, wonderful, beautiful, purified Church in resplendent glory, sharing and shining with the glory that He has given to His Church. Because Jesus says, "The glory, Lord, that You have given to me, I give to them". And we are going to be a glorious Church.

The Great Lurch

And this will be the thing that will make us one. We will be one people. There will be none of this – 'Oh, it's that church', or 'Oh I go to this church,' or 'My church is better than your church' – there will be none of that. Because we will all have the same enemy, we will all have the same fears, we will all have the same problems, and we can only pull through this together. And this will be a time, a great lurch, as this country breaks free from Europe. Because God is going to do it whether we like it or not. And unfortunately, the way it is going to be done is going to be costly to us. But as our nation lurches to one side and everyone falls over, and things start to shake, as we get up and rise up again, we will realise that as Christians, we cannot afford to do things by ourselves. The day of wanting to build a name for myself, or you know, be the next Kathryn Kuhlman, or whatever it is, are over. There is no time for this anymore. There is no time for celebrities anymore. Everything that we know will be gone. The pop idols, all of that, will be meaningless. Nothing. Gone. The only thing that will be idolised in this country will be that which should be idolised, and that is the name of Jesus. Only He will be idolised in these upcoming days.

It is going to be a glorious time, church. It is going to be glorious. But it is going to be difficult, because of the things that we put our trust in. Even things that we don't know we put our trust in. God wants us to trust in Him with all of our hearts. And He wants us to love Him with all of our mind, all of our spirit, all of our soul, and all of our energies. God is not judging us tonight. He is not judging His church. But He is warning us. But He is also encouraging us. Good things are coming. Really good things are coming.

But a time of great shaking has now begun on our nation. And you see, God does not want His people walking around like headless chickens, going [squawking] 'Oh my God! Oh my God! Oh my God!' No, He wants His people to, when the world is going, 'What is going on around here?' – and I am telling you, everything will lurch. You know, what I see in my mind's eye is: Everything lurches so hard and so quick. Buildings are cracking and splitting and things are coming tumbling down, and people are running in panic, wondering what is going on. The institutions of this land are now going to topple. And everyone is going to wonder what on earth is going on. And the only people that should have it together is going to be us. They are going to look to us, and it is like it says in Isaiah. It says, many people will come to the Jew and grab a hold of him and say, you know, 'You have the ways of salvation; you know the way of salvation – tell me! show me!' [Isaiah 2:3; 4:1; Zechariah 8:20-23] And that is what is going to happen. But if you and I are running around like headless chickens, like everybody else...

You can't say you didn't know this was coming. You can't say that you weren't warned. You cannot say it. You cannot, in good conscience, in your heart of hearts, say, 'Well, you know, I just, I never knew that was ever going to happen. I just never thought it was going to happen in my lifetime.' Because you know, deep down in here. You've known it. You've all in this room, everybody has known it. And you knew that the clock was ticking away – tick, tick, tick. Everybody in this room knew it. You might not have realised it was going to be coming so quick. But this has been a long time coming. A long time coming. And I believe God has been gracious to our nation by holding it off as long as He could. But it is here now, and it is here to stay.

A Heart For Britain

And this whole country is going to be a new country. And it is going to be built on the back of prayer. This nation is not going to be built on the back of labourers, or the cleverness or the wisdom of man, or the economies of man. This country will be built on the back of the prayers of the saints. It will be a united church that will bring about this nation's rising again. It will be on the back of this church. This nation... You see, God loves this nation. People have a heart for Israel, and rightly so. But people lack a heart for their own country, and for their own people. And God would have you know that He has a heart for this country. He has a love for this country. He has given our nation history that you should be proud of, a heritage of spirituality that has lasted nearly thousands of years in this country. You should be proud of it. God has an agenda and a plan and a purpose for this seemingly small and insignificant country. And God has not forgotten this country. God has a plan for this country. There have been many great prophecies over this country. This country is significant to the affairs of Israel in the future. God has a plan.

But God wants you to see this land as also as your promised land. God wants you to see this land as your heritage, your fair and green and pleasant land. He wants you to get a heart and a hunger for this nation again. Don't look at it for all the filth, but look at it for what she once was, and what she could be again. Look at it with the eyes of the Spirit. Look at it and go, 'Lord, this is what we contend for in the Spirit! This is what we yearn for! This is what we cry out for! This is what we pray for, Lord God, that You would make this ancient land thrum with the energy of Your Spirit again, Lord God, as the people are praying and the people are praising and the people are worshipping, and there are churches from the top of this land to the very bottom of this land, Lord God, where people are singing and crying out and praying to You, and the land is full of little fires, all over the place, so the whole country is like a burning torch at night, as this whole nation thrums with the very glory of God.'

"You might say, 'This is a load of rubbish!' Well, I would say to you," says the Lord, "read your history. Read your history. I have done it before. And it stands to reason, if I have done it before, I will do it again. For I am unchanging," says the Lord. "I am the same yesterday, and I am the same today. I am the Rock, and I changeth not. If I did it two hundred years ago, I will do it again. But I am going to do it in greater measure. Why? Because there is more at stake. There are more people. I am going to give my church such a heart for the souls of this nation, that I am going to birth a spirit of intercession on my people. But it will be an unnatural spirit of intercession, unnatural for your human body, in that I will enable you to do things in the Spirit that your physical body would not allow you to do. You will have endurance that the physical body could not endure. This will be a supernatural empowering of my people to pray for this nation."

God is going to do some outlandish and crazy things! The things that He is about to do in this nation, what we are going to do, this is how it is going to be: In twenty years' time, we are going to look back and go, 'Man, we were clueless. We just had no idea. We thought we were clever. We knew nothing. We knew nothing! We had no idea that God could do the things that He does now.' Our God is a good God. Amen? ["Amen!"] He has got a plan. He has got a hope for us. Hallelujah. Glory be to God.

Praise you, Jesus. Lord, we praise you, Lord, that You have a heart for this nation, Lord God. You love this nation, Jesus. You love this green and pleasant land. You love this place. You love the heritage she has for You, Lord Jesus. You love, Lord God, the fact that this nation had communities of people that just prayed and worshipped and adored You. You love the fact that the whole of the nation came together in prayer, Lord God, from the evil might of the Germans, Lord God. You came, Lord Jesus, and You delivered us. You love this land, and we praise You for it, Jesus. We give You all the praise, and we give You all the glory. And we pray, O God, let us not be a fearful people, but let us be a triumphant, victorious, brave and strong people." O glory, glory, glory, glory, glory.

Muslims and Persecution

God would also say this: "There will come a persecution, but I will not permit it to get out of hand. You will get persecution, and it will come from the Muslims, but I will not let it get out of hand. I will protect my people, because all that which is shaken will be shaken. You see, as the church provokes my people Israel to jealousy, you will be provoking Muslims to jealousy. You will be provoking them with the reality that your God is real and theirs is not, and they will hate you for it. But I will turn many to come to know me. For I am going to tell you this: I am going to break the back of Islam in this country. I am going to break its back, that it will be a weak, feeble religion. But I am going to do glorious things through those people. But also, church, this is going to be a difficult time, because public opinion is going to move away from the Muslims. At the moment, everyone loves them. But the time is coming when public opinion will despise them. And you see, my church, you have got to be very careful, because you are not allowed to judge or despise anybody. But you must love all of mankind, and you must help the Muslim, as much as you would help the Englishman, as much as you would help the Jew. You must help them. When times of difficulty arise, you must help them! But in doing that, you may incur the wrath of your own country. You have a choice: you either go with your country and incur my wrath, or you do the right thing and you may incur the wrath of your people."

For the Joy Set Before Us...

"These are going to be difficult times, but they are going to be the best of times. It is going to be known as the golden age of the Church, when the Church comes into her fulness. You are going to see things... Well, put it this way, there is no reference point to what you are coming into, no reference point at all. You will look back at ancient revivals and you will not find what you are looking for, because there is no reference point. What is coming is so far beyond anything you have experienced or anything you have ever touched, seen or read or known about, that the revivals of the past will not be your reference point. You will be in the deep end, just as much as they were, but you won't drown."

Hallelujah. So be encouraged. Be blessed, and forewarned. You are prepared. You are God's Bride. He loves you. He delights in you, and He loves you. Guys, He loves us so much. He knows that He has brought a heavy word to us. But what is coming... You see, Jesus set His face like flint. He knew what was coming. But He looked beyond that, because He knew the joys of what was soon to come after that. And that is how we as the Church need to be – set our faces like flint at what is about to come, but look to the joy of what is over the top of that. In Jesus' name, Amen.

Christopher Wickland. Sermon transcript from 25th of November 2018

God will restore the broken and lame

Micah 4:6-7 *'In that Day, says the Lord, I will gather the lame and I will gather the exile and the one whom I have afflicted and I will make the lame a remnant and the exile a strong nation, and the LORD will reign over them on Mount Zion from here on, even forever.'*

I believe the Lord in the days coming will gather the lame, the broken, the damaged and the exiled back into His fold, the church. There are so many disenfranchised believers who have left communities or have even been forced out, sometimes for no fault of their own, other times because of their rebellious hearts.

I sense that God, like a mother hen, wants to put His loving wing over His brood and call back those who have strayed, back to His heart and His people. Some of these prodigals have been afflicted by God for their hardness of heart. Yet we know that God's chastisement is only for a while and that He chastises those whom He loves.

Many of the lame and broken understand that deep within lies an unfulfilled calling and hope. They know that they were destined to do works of service in God's kingdom. Yet they walk in the shadowlands of loss and hopelessness as day by day they sense they are drifting from what they were called to do. This has filled some with bitterness, anger, sadness and regret.

The gifts and callings of God are irrevocable, there is always hope, there is always a fresh start, for His mercies are new every morning. If His people will only humble themselves, turn from their wicked ways and pray, then God will bring healing and restoration. Is not Jehovah Rapha the God who heals? Is He not the God of restoration and restitution?

Remember the parable of the Prodigal son, when he returned home remember what the father did. He put a robe upon his sons body and a ring of inheritance back on his finger. Remember also David's mighty men, for some of them to begin with were malcontents and debtors yet in time they became mighty warriors, men of renown. It is never too late to return home. It is not too late to become all that the Father destined you to be.

God gives His grace to the humble and resists the proud, so we need to be aware that God's invitation and promise is to those who acknowledge they are lame, broken, damaged and exiled. Some need to acknowledge that they had a part to play in the reasons why they became exiled in the first place. Restoration and restitution begins with humility and repentance.

I believe God is saying that there are so many who have left the fold over the years and He wants them to come home. He wishes to kiss you and weep for joy over you, He wants to renew and restore you.

Some may think it's too late, that too much water has gone under the bridge. Yet with God a day is as a thousand years and a thousand years is as one day. Time is irrelevant to our Father in heaven. His hand is reaching out to so many right now, He is imploring all his prodigals to return home.

There is a warning in all this as well. It took a famine to bring the prodigal son to his senses. God will sometimes bring hardships and difficulties into our lives to make us open our eyes and come to the end of our tether. Sometimes we need to hit rock bottom before we get our momentous epiphany.

God is long-suffering and patient and it is this quality that leads many to repentance. Father wants you to know that He has not abandoned you and that He is not far from you. If you call upon His Name He shall surely save you, He will be your shield, and your bulwark.

I believe Father is saying that it's now time for the prodigals to come home. Yes you may have a grumpy brother to return to but he will mellow in time. Be brave, be humble and come back to the place of the Father's heart and love. Come back to God and come back home to His wonderful family.

Chris Wickland 16th of August 2023

God is calling us to the wilderness

Hosea 2:16 &18a & 19 *'Therefore, behold, I AM will lure her and bring her in the wilderness and speak to her heart. And it will be at that day, says the LORD, you will call Me Ishi - My Husband. For I shall take away the names of the Baalim out of her mouth and they will no longer be remembered by their names.'*

This morning as I was reading my bible, I came across the above passage and felt that God wanted to speak to His church. A beautiful message of hope, deliverance and joy.

I believe God is coming to lure His church, His beautiful church, into the place of the wilderness. For He loves His church with such a tender love and I sensed that He weeps for His bride to be, His church, with such yearning.

But what has become of us, the church, God's holy virgin? We are supposed to be keeping ourselves chaste to Him, we are supposed to be always prepared for His returning. We are supposed to be looking our best at all times, for we know not the day or the hour of His return. We are to be washed and perfumed for Jesus our love, we are called to be pure and spotless.

But look at us! We have grown fat, our hair is disheveled, our wedding garments are old and tattered. We are carousing in places where a woman of honour and status should not be frequenting. We wear the cheap perfume of the world and we have stopped looking for His return. In fact many no longer believe He ever will return. We have become faithless and we have broken our beloved's heart.

I believe that God will be bringing His church into the wilderness, but with a heart of love. For even though we look a mess, God still sees the beauty of His church and how beautiful she will yet become. We have grown too reliant upon ourselves and our own ideas, we have become rich, fat and lazy.

I believe God is going to lure us, His church into the wilderness, where He is going to show us His love and refine us. In that wilderness we shall again look to Him, and He will tenderly look after us, as He did for Israel in the wilderness those forty years.

As He strips away the distractions, I believe we will in time grow tired of looking at the desert, and then finally we will lift our eyes up to Him. We will be ashamed in that day for what we have become, but knowing that He loves us with a tender love and that He will restore us. He will never fail or forsake His people. He will tenderly feed us with His sweet bread from heaven. He will teach us again His ways and His precepts. Our hearts will burn again with sweet love for Him. We will learn to raise our hands in true prayer and worship once again. We will re-clothe ourselves and wash our filthy garments. The church will again learn to eagerly desire and await His return, as the church once did at the beginning.

In the place of the wilderness we will again call Jesus, husband. In the place of the wilderness we will understand what it means to be, 'The Bride of Christ.' We will put away our crusades and idols of the day. We will burn them and grind them to dust. Never again will we bow down before the spirit of the age and never again will we embrace false gods and philosophies. We will be besotted by Him, the One True God, we will love His ways, His statutes and His ordinances.

When the church comes to this place and we call Him, 'My beloved,' then and only then will He return to take us to His kingdom where we shall consummate our love for one another.

I believe God is saying these words 'My bride, My people, hasten My return by your love for Me.'

Christopher Wickland 21st of August 2023

I also have sheep that are not from this sheepfold

John 10:16 *'But I also have sheep that are not from this sheepfold: and it is necessary for Me to lead those and they will hear My voice, and they will become one flock.'*

I need to make something very clear to my church, the sheepfold of the Gentiles and Jews was as radical in its day as the bringing together of Catholics and Protestants will be in the days ahead.

This is My heart for the Global Church, and I want this in the United Kingdom. The Reformation is over and it is time to move toward a Re-formation. This is not merely about bringing the divorced parties back together again. No, rather this time I want there to do something fresh and beautiful. I want to take the best from both ends of the spectrum and make them form a oneness, a plural unity. As I am a plural unity, so I want Catholics and Protestants to form a plural unity. In other words one does not lose its identity within the other. I don't want assimilation, I want a marriage and a joining together.

I want a synergy to take place, where the two denominations produce a combined effect greater than the sum of their separate parts. I want to blend the ancient with the modern. That is to say, the ancient paths and ways of the ancient church, holding together in tension and resolution with the modern church (post reformation).

There is a strength and beauty between the two great denominations which only a few are brave enough to see across that great divide. But I am going to do a new thing, one which is new and at the same time, not new. Something that will raise the eyebrows of many. This synergy is going to happen, no matter how much men and women fight, kick and scream against it (for many will). Many will claim this is a work of Satan trying to bring yet further division into My church, but this is not so.

Many will say, 'We don't need yet another denomination!' However, this is a first fruit, a thing of beauty which shall rise from the ash of the great denominations as My chastisement falls. Your wineskins are old and tough, you have become inflexible and hard hearted.

I am going to hand pick a select few to start this new movement, at first it will start very small and many will mock it. But then it will grow and grow and then mockery will turn to fear (for some) and fear to hatred. What some perceive to be going backward is actually My heart, My will, My plans and My purposes for this nation and others. This is a part of the big picture, this is My heart and My will.

Have you not asked Me what I want and what I desire? For this is My desire and My heart and what I want and purpose to come to pass, no matter the conflict it may cause.

This move will bring much joy to many, but equally distress and consternation to others. Many will fight and do all in their power to put down this move and try to stamp it out with theology and zealous passion. Yet, this is My plans and purposes and no one will stop it. Indeed the harder one tries to stop this, the more fuel you will add to the fire and the greater it will become.

Many in the Catholic and Protestant churches will want to entrench themselves according to the old ways and not move forward. They will set up the old divisions to try to protect themselves and stop what I am going to do. But I am going to bring many Protestants and Catholics together and they are going to form something new and fresh. Something which has the power and authority of My name for the days ahead. This new movement will be so beautiful that it will attract many to her fold.

This new movement will not be without its foibles, errors and problems and will require great men and women of calibre to form new liturgies, prayer books and creeds. There will be a need to create balance and also the place of holding things in tension theologically. I want the best of the modern and the best of the ancient to come together and form a plural unity, a plural one, Just as I AM one. I AM three persons yet I AM One.

I will help with this movement, I will place a great Spirit of wisdom to build this tabernacle with skill and wonder. I will place the power of My Spirit in this movement also. For where brothers dwell together in unity, there I command the blessing of life forevermore.

This prophecy will hang on the walls of many and will be a hope and promise that I AM doing this. Many will see, wonder and marvel at whether this word shall come to pass. But it surely shall come to pass.

Christopher Wickland 12th of September 2023

The marrying of the two great houses

Ezekiel 37:15-19. *'The word of Yahweh came to me in these terms, "Son of man, take a piece of wood and write on it: Judah and the Israelites LOYAL TO HIM. Take another piece of wood and write: Joseph, the branch of Ephraim, and the Israelites LOYAL TO HIM.' Join one to another to make a single pice of wood in your hand. When your people say to you, 'Won't you tell us what this means?' Say to them: Yahweh says this: I am going to take the branch of Joseph, which is in the hand of Ephraim , and the tribes of Isreal loyal to him, and put Judah's branch with them; and they will be as one in my hand.'*

In the days ahead, I am wanting to do a bold and daring new thing. I want to bring two old houses back together again to form a new large house. This is something I am going to do here in the United Kingdom. Indeed it has already begun, but it is below the surface for now.

In time I will call a brave remnant from within each house to accomplish this. Where they will come together and form something new and wonderful, yet somehow ancient, all at the same time. In the past I have spoken in riddles on this matter, but now I am going to state it clearly. I want my people to re-form!

It is time to put aside your petty differences and stop refusing to be one people. It is time to stop justifying war in My house. I am not happy with some of you, some who perpetuate old war stories of a bygone age. People who justify hatred and suspicion amongst My children. People who think they are justified in spreading the excrement of hatred and fear among the field of My church. How very dare you! This is My house, not yours! Be very mindful christian. Do not be like the pharisees who were more interested in their religion and sectarianism than they were in My kingdom. Do not find yourself guilty of the same sin.

I am going to birth a first fruit church in this nation, a bringing together of the two great houses. The Catholics and the Protestants. This will not be one coming back under another. Rather this will be a marriage of equals. They will love and respect each other as such. This will be a true blending of the ancient and the modern. This marriage will be a powerful alliance, yet one which will be despised by the parents of both sides.

The parents do not want this marriage and they will fight it and cruel will be their fight. Yet what I have brought together, let no man bring asunder. This will surely come to pass. For the love these two houses have for one another will be great.

I will raise a few brave souls from within these two houses, ones who are faithful to Me and this calling. They will come together and form such a beautiful bond that they will have no choice but to marry. When this marriage takes place there will be much rejoicing in heaven, yet much consternation will be upon the earth because of it.
Many will claim this is a work of the Devil. Many will use all in their power to undo this movement. But all will be to no avail. For the love the two houses have for each other will be too strong, because My hand has made it so.

As I brought Jew and Gentile together, so I will bring many from these great houses back together. Oh many will cry and lament how such a thing could possibly be. Well, watch and see. For this will surely come to pass and it will start small but then like a tender shoot, will grow into a powerful oak tree in this land. I will put a blazing sword around this tree and none shall be permitted to chop it down. It will grow and in time will be accepted by the other great trees in the orchard of My kingdom.

Christopher Wickland 1st of October 2023

The cutting down of the Sycamore Gap tree in Hadrian's wall on September 28th 2023

The great Sycamore Gap tree of England has been chopped down! The tree of Robin Hood has gone, its iconic stature now vanished from the vista of northern England. Everyone is calling it an act of senseless vandalism and that is exactly what it is.

Daniel 4:23 *'And inasmuch as the king saw a watcher, a holy one, coming down from heaven and saying, 'Chop down the tree and destroy it, but leave its stump and roots in the earth, bound with a band of iron and bronze in the tender grass of the field; let it be wet with the dew of heaven, and let him graze with the beasts of the field, till seven times pass over him.'*

The chopping down of this tree (I believe) is a symbol of the senseless vandalism that the bishops have brought upon the Church of England. They have rejected God's word and replaced it with their own. They have taken that once great institution and wreaked havoc upon it and the souls within her.

I believe the Lord is saying that the church of England will be removed for a time, times and half a time from the wider Anglican Communion. She will be greatly humbled and brought low, she will be chopped down and her status removed. That great British icon of a church and institution will be greatly humbled and removed from the sight of many, only a stump will remain.

However in time new shoots will arise from the stump and in time a new sycamore will rise from the debris of the fallen. Something beautiful will arise and it will be permitted to grow quickly. This new sycamore will hold great hope for the future, yet she will never come back to her former glory. However, she will be permitted to grow again within God's orchard.

For those within this church I believe God is saying, 'do not despair.' Even though more woe is coming, hold fast and stay true. God will restore and rebuild from the faithful remnant that remain. I also feel God is saying that He has called Many into the Church of England to help her and rescue her.   Be assured of this calling. Even though it looks like so much will be lost. Stand strong and hope in God, for you will see the goodness of God in the land of the living.

Christopher Wickland 2nd of October 2023

143

Other books by chris Wickland

Returning to the abbey of the Holy Ghost
Advent Reflections
The biblical importance of Israel
Ten biblical steps to freedom
Hidden gems of Torah
Basic Doctrine (Book 1)
The blessing of Abraham

To watch or listen to
Chris Wickland's sermons and prophetic words,
please check out his YouTube cannel
'Storehouse 7.'

For Chris Wickland's podcasts please go to any
podcasting platform and search under
'Storehouse 7.'

Printed in Great Britain
by Amazon

41c100cd-178a-4cf3-8eea-b0d27c1ecbc3R01